Assessment
for
Learning
in
Higher
Education

The Staff and Educational Development Series
Series Editor: Sally Brown

Assessing Competence in Higher Education Edited by Anne Edwards and
  Peter Knight

Assessment for Learning in Higher Education Edited by Peter Knight

Research, Teaching and Learning in Higher Education Edited by Brenda Smith
  and Sally Brown

SEDA is the Staff and Educational Development Association. It supports
and encourages developments in teaching and learning in higher
education through a variety of methods: publications, conferences, net-
working, journals, regional meetings and research – and through the
SEDA Fellowship Scheme. Further details may be obtained from:

The SEDA administrator
Gala House
3 Raglan Road
Edgbaston
Birmingham B5 7RA
Tel: 0121-440 5021
Fax: 0121-440 5022

Assessment for Learning

in

Higher Education

EDITED BY
PETER KNIGHT

KOGAN
PAGE

Published in association with the
Staff and Educational Development Association

First published in 1995

Apart from any fair dealing for the purposes of research or private study, or criticism or review, as permitted under the Copyright, Designs and Patents Act, 1988, this publication may only be reproduced, stored or transmitted, in any form or by any means, with the prior permission in writing of the publishers, or in the case of reprographic reproduction in accordance with the terms of licences issued by the Copyright Licensing Agency. Enquiries concerning reproduction outside those terms should be sent to the publishers at the undermentioned address:

Kogan Page Limited
120 Pentonville Road
London N1 9JN

© Peter Knight and named contributors, 1995

British Library Cataloguing in Publication Data

A CIP record for this book is available from the British Library.

ISBN 0 7494 1532 0

Typeset by DP Photosetting, Aylesbury, Bucks
Printed and bound in Great Britain by
Biddles Ltd, Guildford and King's Lynn.

Contents

Notes on Contributors

Madeleine Atkins is Senior Lecturer in Educational Management at the University of Newcastle upon Tyne and Head of the Department of Education. She has a long-standing interest in research on teaching and learning in higher education and in staff development. With George Brown she wrote *Effective Teaching in Higher Education*.

David Boud is Professor of Adult Education at the University of Technology, Sydney. He is a long-time proponent of the need to appraise academic practices, including assessment, in terms of how students see them and of their impact upon student learning. Amongst his many publications are *Appreciating Adults Learning, Reflection: Turning experience into learning, The Challenge of Problem-based Learning* and a large number of articles, including ones on assessment and self-assessment.

Sally Brown is based in the Educational Development Service at the University of Northumbria at Newcastle. She is Chair of the SEDA publications committee and runs staff development workshops in the UK and overseas. She has written extensively on educational development and teaching issues. Recent books include *Assessing Learners in Higher Education* and *Research, Teaching and Learning in Higher Education*.

Phyllis Creme is involved both in educational development and in Film Studies teaching at the University of North London. She is based in the university's Centre for Higher Education and Access Development and has responsibility for teaching and learning innovation.

Kate Day is the Research and Development Officer and **Dai Hounsell** is the Director of the Centre for Teaching, Learning and Assessment at the University of Edinburgh. They work collaboratively in a number of areas, including feedback and evaluation, quality assurance, and assessment. Dai is coordinator for a large-scale project on assessment strategies in Scottish higher education, in which Kate is involved as a Project Director.

T Dary Erwin is Director of the Office of Student Assessment at James Madison University, Virginia and Professor of Psychology. His published works include the recent *Assessing Student Learning and Development*.

Nancy Falchikov works in the Department of Social Sciences at Napier University, Edinburgh. In addition to self- and peer-assessment, her research interests include the effects on student learning of matches and mismatches in the learning environment in terms of student approaches to learning, methods of teaching and assessment practices.

Bob Farmer and **Diana Eastcott** work in the Learning Methods Unit at the University of Central England in Birmingham. They are both practising teachers, trainers, educational consultants and authors of a wide range of articles on teaching and learning.

Hazel Fullerton has used her design training in posts in video production and training; in setting up resource-based learning in schools; as a communications tutor in Further Education; and as a technology tutor/counsellor with the Open University. She is now Academic Staff Development Coordinator at the University of Plymouth.

Romla Hadrill works at the Manchester Metropolitan University in the field of post-compulsory teacher education. Current work includes consultancy for the CVCP Staff Development Unit on a project that is mapping higher-level NVQs and the work of staff in higher education. She is vice-chair of the Universities Professional Development Consortium for post-compulsory education and training and a lay inspector for the Further Education Funding Council.

Irene Harris is Senior Lecturer in the Faculty of Management and Business at the Manchester Metropolitan University. Her interest in assessment issues has been fuelled by her work with students, her own experience as a mature student and by being a manager of an Enterprise in Higher Education project.

Peter Knight is a lecturer in Lancaster University's Department of Educational Research.

Ivan Moore is currently Assistant Director of Educational Development at the University of Ulster. A Fellow of SEDA, he acts as a consultant on teaching, learning and educational development, about which he has also written three books and a number of papers.

Phil Race is Professor of Educational Development at the University of Glamorgan. His interest in assessment stems from many years as an examiner and from work helping students to improve their learning strategies and communication techniques. An active author and consultant, his most recent books include *500 Tips for Students* and *500 Tips for Tutors*.

Chris Rust is Principal Lecturer in the Educational Methods Unit of Oxford Brookes University. Through the Oxford Centre for Staff Development, he regularly runs workshops around the country on issues such as assessment. He is co-author of *Strategies for Diversifying Assessment* and has edited two successful induction packs for new lecturers.

Note: Many of the publications mentioned here were written by more than one author. To keep this snappy, I've generally not mentioned these co-authors.

Preface

The assessment of student learning has often been seen as a tiresome and harmful necessity. Tiresome, because of the amount of work it imposed upon learners and tutors and because it seemed to get in the way of worthwhile learning; harmful because it seemed to encourage cramming, superficiality and conformity; and a necessity because without it there was no way for universities to show that they maintained high standards. Besides, without assessment, what was there to make students work?

An alternative view has emerged in schools and higher education, namely that 'student assessment is at the heart of an integrated approach to student learning' (Harvey, 1993, p.10). It is becoming appreciated that assessment arrangements can be diverse; can support ambitious curriculum aims; and can foster understanding. So far from there being a tension between assessment and learning, reformed assessment arrangements might be a necessary condition for better student learning to take place.

In this belief, the Staff and Educational Development Association (SEDA) organized a conference in May 1994 around the theme of assessment for better student learning. The chapters in this collection constitute a selection of the 32 conference presentations. All have been rewritten for this book, although Dary Erwin's chapter (Chapter 3) was especially written for this book.

While I have dealt with the mechanics of editing, I am indebted to colleagues for their academic help in planning the collection. First comes Sue Drew, of Sheffield Hallam University, who was a vigorous and efficient conference organizer, leading the SEDA conference planning committee. That committee also comprised Joyce Barlow of the University of Brighton, Richard Kemp of the University of Glamorgan and Ranald MacDonald of Sheffield Hallam University. It benefited from the support of Jill Brookes, SEDA administrator and Jessica Claridge of the University of Exeter. At the conference I was grateful to the following for their advice: Dr Liz Beaty of the University of Brighton, Ms Sally Brown of the University of Northumbria at Newcastle, Professor Arnold Goldman of the University of Kent, Professor Phil Race of the University of

Glamorgan and Mr Chris Rust of Oxford Brookes University. Three of these people have papers in this collection but they were not party to their selection.

Peter Knight, March 1995

Introduction

Peter Knight

ASSESSMENT – EVIDENCE OF QUALITY

Assessment is a moral activity. What we choose to assess and how shows quite starkly what we value. In assessing *these* aspects of chemistry or by assessing German in *that* way, we are making it abundantly clear what we value in *this* programme and in higher education in general. So, if we choose not to assess general transferable skills, then it is an unambiguous sign that promoting them is not seen to be an important part of our work and of our programme. That position is, of course, defensible in several ways, not least on the grounds that these skills (whatever 'skills' might be) may not be quite so general, let alone easily transferable (see Eraut, 1994b and Atkins, this volume). Yet, whether the intellectual position is defensible or not, in choosing not to assess learners' general transferable skills through these programmes we reveal our values.

And we reveal them quite starkly. In writing a mission statement, a programme plan or a validation document, skilled drafting allows us to lay claim to a wonderland of concepts, skills, competences and the like, of which our students are to be made citizens. But for those who want to know about the quality of a course, programme or institution, the test is whether these goals are assessed and how well they are assessed. In a sense, the way students are assessed is the 'DNA evidence' of their learning experiences. We might say that we have been trying to promote these skills, understanding in that area, or competence in this element but if there is no evidence of appropriate assessment, then the DNA evidence belies the claim. At best, the absence of assessment suggests that our intentions have not been completely realized. At worst, it says that our intentions were rhetorical, for the benefit of auditors, not students.

To illustrate some of the things that might be inferred about a university and its attitude to student learning from assessment data, I want to look at the University of Arcadia, which could be in Wigan, Weymouth or Wolvercote. Fictional though the university is, the data come from real, unpublished case studies.

ARCADIA AND ASSESSMENT

At Arcadia the same degree may be gained through courses offered by different teams which work on different sites. The courses have very different assessment requirements. It has only been possible to look at written work that contributes to degree classification, but the picture of assessment demands is quite striking, as Table I.1 shows.

At the very least there is a moral issue here about the differential requirements upon learners who will all end up with a University of Arcadia degree. This unease about the fairness of the system might be compounded by data showing that in the year in which these data were collected, 60 per cent of students on BA course 3 graduated with an upper second or first class honours degree, even though they had

Table I.1   *A comparison of assessment requirements for some post-Year 1 students at the University of Arcadia*

Degree title	Number of coursework items	Total length of coursework (words)	Dissertation requirement (words)	Length of examinations (hours)
Education, subject 1, course A	18	43,000	optional	24
Education, subject 1, course B	23	50,000	compulsory, 10,000+	17
Education, subject 2, course A	Not clear in validation documents	Not clear in validation documents	optional	21
Education, subject 2, course B	Not clear in validation documents	50,500	compulsory, 10,000+	12
BA, subject 1, course A	10	21,000	compulsory, 10,000+	13
BA, subject 1, course B	22	40,000	compulsory, 10,000+	16
BA, subject 2, course A	16	32,000	compulsory, 10,000+	16
BA, subject 2, course B	13–15	39,000	optional	18

entered the course with modest 'A' level scores (a mean of just under 11 points). Students entering another BA course had lower mean 'A' level scores (just over nine points) but only 13 per cent of them got an upper second or first class honours degree. Those entering with the best 'A' level scores took yet another BA course but just 42 per cent got an upper second or first class honours degree. This odd pattern cannot be simply attributed to the assessment procedures in use, for the quality of teaching might have played an important part.

A closer examination of validation documents drawn from a sample of eight departments at Arcadia shows further diversity between departments, this time in variations in the balance between assessment through coursework and by examination; in the amount of assessed work required by different departments; in the form of assessment items; and in the timing of assessment. Students taking joint honours degrees would often be assessed quite differently in the two strands of their degree. What the validation documents had in common was a reliance on a narrow range of assessment methods; silence about assessment criteria; an absence of plans to assess 'core competences' or 'general, transferable skills'; and a general indifference to self- and peer-assessment.

So, what defines a degree from this ubiquitous university? The answer seems to be that only indifferent assessment practices cut across the proliferation of diversity. Survival of the fittest has not operated here: rather, perhaps, survival of the flattest – those assessment arrangements which are least likely to jolt the passage of traditional, well-oiled teaching and learning juggernauts.

A study of students at Arcadia showed that departmental codes of practice had a lot to say about the bureaucracy of assessment but little about the purposes and criteria of assessment and that,

> students often don't know why the system is as it is, or how they are meant to do something. Basic questions remain unanswered, for example, 'What skills am I being assessed on?', 'Why do we have exams?' Students have numerous doubts regarding the *reliability, validity and effectiveness* of assessment, as well as the degree to which it *contributes to the learning process.*

Another study found that students doing dissertations were not sure about the purpose of doing so and were often quite intimidated by the process of coping with this form of assessment. A third study found that the quality of feedback on assessed work left much to be desired, especially since it was usually slow to arrive and so bound to the specifics of the task in hand that it failed to offer much useful, general advice for doing better on the next task.

These data would be consistent with a view that at Arcadia assessment was a vital ritual in the maintenance of some hazy features of the social order. They would not seem to be so consistent with the common sense view that assessment was designed to buttress students' learning. If that is so, it would appear that Arcadia is ripe for an anthropological study.

Examination of the marks attained by students on each unit of assessment shows some interesting features. In each of three non-natural science departments studied, coursework marks are higher than examination marks across a two-year period. The largest mean difference is nearly seven marks and the smallest is just over one. Clearly, the assessment system is working against those who are better at examinations than at coursework, which may be desirable but which also is an expression of certain educational values.

Those who chose to take examinations during the second year had mean scores that were about 1.5 per cent lower than their third-year examination marks, although coursework marks for second-year work were not statistically significantly different from third-year coursework marks. This might make us wonder about the wisdom of modularization with its emphasis on completing unit assessment when the unit itself is completed. It might also make us wonder about the claim that students develop in their third year. If their coursework improves, then these marks do not show it!

Similarly for data showing that women outperform men in these subjects: their mean coursework score is nearly four marks higher than the men's, while the mean examination score is nearly three marks higher. Is this to be interpreted as showing that the assessment system is unfair to men, or that teaching and learning do not sufficiently engage men, or that women taking those subjects in those years were simply cleverer?

Examinations have a long history and it might be assumed that a certain objectivity attaches to the information they provide. However, at Arcadia we can see variations in the performance of different groups of students that would seem to need some reasoned justification. None appears to be to hand, although Erwin, in Chapter 3 of this volume, is clear that in a North American setting such variations would be probed and an account would be called for. But most North American universities have assessment offices and take assessment much more seriously (in many ways) than do their British counterparts. One consequence is that they actually have to hand detailed data about student performance that can be centrally analysed in all sorts of ways. In the UK, data tend to be held locally, with university administrations often holding only the most bland of data, of little value even if they were disposed to ask some awkward questions about the actual operation of the validated assessment system.

The point of this account of assessment practices at Arcadia is not to claim that there is anything particularly unusual there, except only that unusual interest seems to have been taken in finding out what is happening within the assessment system. The point is that existing assessment systems, such as Arcadia's, advantage some learners and disadvantage others; reward some forms of achievement and not others; and seem to do so in eclectic ways, without evidence of any unifying rhyme or reason. Proponents of new approaches to assessment should have to account for the values that are being promoted by their innovations, for by promoting *these* values they are narrowing the scope within which *those* values can operate. However, it is not a contest between the innovators' values and an existing, morally-neutral system. Rather, the present system is as open to moral objection as any other and perhaps, because of its seemingly ramshackle nature, it is more open to objection.

OVERVIEW OF THE BOOK

As Madeleine Atkins says in Chapter 1, these arguments hinge on what we expect higher education to do:

> Inescapably, the issues are about what students are learning and who is going to define it. And the answers cannot just be in terms of rather low-level generic skills and competences if higher education is to justify its costly existence in the twenty-first century. There also has to be a debate about the knowledge and understanding that one should expect a student to gain from an undergraduate programme, unfashionable though such a debate has been for some time....

It is a truism that effective assessment depends upon having a view of what it is that we are trying to do in a programme, hence of what it is that we ought to assess. What is distinctive and important about this chapter is the crisp review of four competing claims about the purpose of higher education. In the process of reviewing them, she notices a number of awkward questions about the development of expertise, the notion of the reflective practitioner and the validity of the concept of 'general transferable skills', for example. The general thrust is that too many claims about the contribution of higher education have been founded on rhetoric rather than on careful analysis with attention to appropriate evidence. In this respect her chapter might usefully be read alongside Barnett's (1994) stimulating views on the nature of higher education.

Arguing that higher education should probably be aiming to provide a general educational experience of intrinsic worth in its own right and to

prepare students for general employment, she recognizes that this position has considerable implications for teaching methods, assessment
issues and staff training. These, though, are second-order matters. First,
we need greater clarity about what we are trying to do through higher
education and that clarity ought to be a product of the application of our
analytical and critical powers, not a result of their absence. One conclusion that might be drawn from the case of the University of Arcadia is
that clarity of purpose is lacking, which can be discerned in the assessment arrangements, which seem to have been hardly touched by the
Enterprise in Higher Education Project money that has flowed through
the university.

David Boud concentrates on what assessment systems do to learners,
which is a recurring theme in this book (see Chapters 4 and 6, for
example). He uses the concept of consequential validity ('the effect of
the test or other form of assessment on learning and other educational
matters') in examining ways in which assessment systems help or hinder
the types of learning that we say we wish to encourage. 'Assessment', he
says, 'is the most significant prompt for learning'; it 'acts as a mechanism
to control students that is far more pervasive and insidious than most staff
would be prepared to acknowledge'. Unfortunately, academic staff are
not as sensitive as they might be to the way assessment seems when seen
through student eyes. 'Even successful, able and committed students ...
have been hurt by their experiences of assessment, time and time again'.
Nor is it enough for any one academic to try to mitigate such effects, for,

> in any given month they [students] may have to complete ten
> assessment tasks, in another month only one. The ways in which they
> approach each of these will be influenced by the others ... Very little
> attention has been given to the compounding effects of assessment.

Looked at in this way, assessment reform is not simply something for
enthusiastic academics to undertake, but is a matter for departmental
and institutional action, which also follows from the arguments
developed in Chapter 1. Illustrations of university-wide approaches to
assessment reform are to be found in Chapters 7–9.

Yet, action by individual academics is important. To repeat a cliché,
effective change is simultaneously 'bottom-up' and 'top-down', a combination of tinkering and radical overhaul. Take the language of assessment as an example. Boud observes that the language of assessment is
often excessively judgemental; 'it has the final say. It classifies without
recourse to reconsideration or further data. And it does not allow for
further possibilities'. 'We judge too much and too powerfully, not
realizing the extent to which students experience our power over them'.

While raising awareness of this problem is best done on an institution- and department-wide basis, individual academics can contribute a lot by reappraising their practice and experimenting with better ways of giving feedback to students.

Dary Erwin is the Director of the Office of Assessment at James Madison University, Virginia. Such offices are to be found in most American universities, signalling a university commitment to taking seriously the assessment of student learning and of the learning experience. Like Boud, he is interested in the relationship between assessment and learning but he approaches the issue from an account- ability and course improvement perspective. There is, he observes, a crisis in assessment, so that,

> grade inflation, awarding grades based on effort and not perfor- mance, uneven standards among instructors or among institutions, and a lack of understanding or agreement about education itself have led to a lack of credible measures.

Echoing Madeleine Atkins, he insists that 'often the lack of clarity in objectives, purposes, competences, or whatever term one wishes to use, causes confusion about what is in the curriculum'.

Despite these internal problems, it is imperative for universities to be able to produce valid and reliable assessment data to demonstrate their value at a time when it is increasingly difficult to secure state resources, and in order to undertake well-informed programme development so as to enhance the student learning experience. His conclusion is that,

> to ignore calls for accountability is to encourage people external to higher education to establish their standards rather than ours. Our response is more critical now than ever. And the credibility of our response depends to a large degree on the adequacy of the assess- ment process we have in place.

It is a conclusion that cannot be ignored anywhere in the anglophone world.

In Chapter 4, Phil Race offers a variety of checklists to help academics, managers, funding councils, quality auditors and policy-makers to scrutinize existing assessment practice in the areas for which they have responsibility. These lists represent the pooled wisdom of delegates to the SEDA conference and as such carry the authority of massed expertise. This authority is enhanced by the data presented in the first part of the chapter, which go a long way to affirm points made in Chapter 2. These delegates, academically and professionally successful people (one trusts), have nightmares about being assessed; have more negative feelings about exams and coursework than they do positive ones, even though they must, as academics, know the case *for* assessment; thought that there is little learning pay-off from examinations; and had concerns about both examinations and coursework assessment. Comparison of these data with the four-fold model of learning which Race advances suggests that assessment practices are, at best, not helping the learning process and, at worst, injurious to it.

Race has also contributed to Chapter 5, in which Chris Rust and Sally Brown briskly discuss a number of questions that might be asked about assessment if we were to take heed of the points made in the previous four chapters and critically appraise its fitness for purpose. They too emphasize the importance of clarity of purpose but they make a point of saying that this must be a *shared* clarity. Learners need to understand the criteria by which their work will be judged every bit as much as do the tutors – arguably more so. After all, assessment is 'an engine for learning'.

This process can be helped by peer- and self-assessment, which are assessment modes that are also valuable on other grounds, such as efficiency. Boud is recognized as a leading proponent of self-assessment as a way of fostering learner autonomy and Brown, Race and Rust follow other contributors to this book in endorsing this position. It seems as though self- and peer- assessment are ideas whose time has now come.

The importance of good feedback is also stressed (and this is a theme that is revisited in Chapter 12), and Records of Achievement, or profiles, are identified as a way in which the meanings of tutors' judgements and of students' perspectives may be brought together and, through negotiation, worked into plans for future personal development within a programme of study. As with Boud, these writers are concerned that through assessment 'the tutor can make learners feel powerless', given 'the seemingly arbitrary nature of tutor assessment' and consider ways in which assessment processes might begin to 'empower' the learner.

This is also a theme of Chapter 6 by Bob Farmer and Diana Eastcott, who adopt Race's model of learning in their review of ways in which assessment might be used to enhance the quality of the student learning experience. As a drawing-together chapter, this endorses much that has gone before but adds to that material examples of practices in use, places greater emphasis on portfolios as a method of formative assessment and draws on Kolb's learning cycle in considering ways of helping students to reflect upon their own learning. Their conclusion, that ' "How am I going to be tested?" is often at the very heart of students' approaches to and feelings about learning', stands as a summary of the main thrust of these first six chapters.

The same themes are woven through the next six chapters, although these chapters are more in the nature of reports of work that has been or is being done on assessment, rather than being analyses of the place and attributes of assessment systems in general.

Ivan Moore describes a rare example of a university-wide approach to assessment reform prompted, interestingly enough, by a feeling that too few first-class degrees were being awarded. His study offers an interesting complement to the case developed in a recent SEDA paper on staff development and university-wide change (Knight, 1994), showing how assessment, teaching and learning are intertwined and that action is necessary at all levels of a university. This makes for a demanding job for the staff developer, although, as Moore points out, this particular project offers greater leverage on educational development than would many others. He presents estimates of the time-cost of the programme that suggest that it will prove to be a very efficient way of provoking significant thinking about the university's teaching and of supporting changes, especially in assessment practices. The following long-term benefits are anticipated:

- changes in course design

- long-term change

- staff will be better informed to continue to improve their assessment practices.

At the University of Plymouth, change agents were used to stimulate assessment reform. An interesting feature, described by Hazel Fullerton in Chapter 8, was an emphasis on using visual media as a way of sharing the development of thinking about assessment reform and then sharing the conclusions with others. This process is succinctly described and five examples are given of posters produced at Plymouth. While the spur to this development was increasing student numbers, the combination of a 'bottom-up' strategy and support from senior management appears to have worked so well that seven developments in assessment practice are now embedded within the university.

Kate Day and Dai Hounsell describe their programme to help part-time graduate tutors to assess better. This, as they remark, is an issue of considerable importance, since some universities are divesting more and more teaching to untrained graduate assistants so that full-time staff can concentrate on the research selectivity exercise. In Chapter 9 they discuss the problems which face staff and educational development personnel when they try to help such a diverse group of people to develop their skill at assessing student learning. Prudently, they conclude that only so much can be done on a university-wide basis, while still insisting that, it is difficult to see how from the viewpoints of quality and accountability universities can avoid setting firm and explicit institution-wide boundaries ... and thus provide more robust policy and practical frameworks within which course and departmental tailoring can be constructively accommodated.

The interplay of assessment and learning is explored in Chapter 10 by Phyllis Creme. She argues that one result of changes at the margins of course assessment requirements has been that 'group discussions have become a more explicit and structured part of the course', with evidence of students taking greater responsibility for their learning. However, the issue of control, raised in Chapters 2 and 4, was not resolved, for while 'students were being expected to take more responsibility than previously for the seminar process', assessment was still something done to them, so that they 'can hardly be expected to be open – or adult – in their attitudes to knowledge if they are not, in the end, allowed to take responsibility for assessing it'.

Similar themes are explored by Irene Harris in Chapter 11, who investigates assessment issues attaching to the use of learning contracts. While learning contracts promise a more equal relationship between learners and tutors, the promise works out quite differently on the three courses that she studied: 'the actual [assessment] situation for individual learners may be very different to the outward experience'. 'Letting go', she added, quoting Tomkins and McGraw (1988, p. 177), 'is sometimes the greatest challenge for the teacher'. So, if learning contracts are to make good their promise, both teachers and students will need to learn new skills.

One of those skills, foreshadowed by Chapters 10 and 11, is that of peer-assessment, which readily shades into self-assessment. Yet peer-assessment causes much concern in some quarters. In Chapter 12, Nancy Falchikov describes her approach to using peer-assessment to improve the quality and speed of feedback to students. Her conclusions were that students' marks were closely aligned with tutors' marks; that motivation benefited; that students were inclined to use tentative language in their comments (Chapter 2, q.v.); and that students were required to use reflection and engage in critical analysis. However, 'it sometimes appeared that only when seminar delivery was good or adequate did students look beyond it to issues of structure and content'. This might suggest that unless students are progressively helped to become more perceptive in their analyses, then peer feedback marking and associated assessment methods will prove to be useful only for assessing the surface features of presentations, which would severely limit the appeal of these widely promoted approaches (see Chapter 5, for example).

This is a salutary reminder that many ideas that are recommended as ways of improving assessment practices have face validity (they look sensible) but they are not supported by the range of systematic and well-designed studies that would allow greater confidence to be placed in them. Perhaps this is inevitable in these early days of reforming assessment in the interests of better learning. Writing of research into school examining, Wood (1991, p. 245) wondered whether 'it is only when a change is announced, preparations for it are made and awareness is raised that serious research becomes possible'. Moreover, 'if it is clear that innovation is not driven by research, and that the reverse may frequently be true, there remain some pointed questions about innovation that beg to be explored' (p. 248). Indeed. As I write this introduction I am conscious on the one hand of the enormous interest in and creativity about assessment and, on the other, by how very little we know, even in the University of Arcadia (but perhaps not at James Madison University), about the effects of assessment on learners, as well as on learning, teaching and teachers.

The National Council for Vocational Qualifications is an example of a political innovation that called forth an enormous amount of research to shape, underpin and refine National Vocational Qualifications (NVQs) and General National Vocational Qualifications (GNVQs). This work has enormous significance for higher education, as Romla Hadrill explains in the final chapter. Acknowledging that there are ideological and technical disputes surrounding the NCVQ's work (see also Barnett, 1994; Eraut, 1994b; Hodkinson and Issitt, 1994; Hyland, 1994; Tomlinson and Saunders, 1995), she none the less sets out the thrust of this work. Higher education would be unwise to assume that NVQs and GNVQs can be ignored. First, the approach to assessment of specifying learning outcomes and then proceeding to assess learners' competence against them will not go away. Moreover, the development of various accreditation and credit accumulation schemes implies that some universities will be interested in recognizing competence that has not been developed through university courses, which is a basic NCVQ principle. Lastly, NVQs have already been developed to levels of achievement equivalent to university work and GNVQs are to be developed to these levels. Not only may these developments have a direct influence on higher education but it is a small step to the idea of a core curriculum for higher education based around the development of certain key competences.

This takes us back to Madeleine Atkins's fundamental questions. What is higher education for? So what are we to assess, given that assessment is a moral activity? To these another two, which have been an undertone throughout this introduction, might be added: What data are available about the effects of different forms of assessment upon different groups of students? And are these data good enough?

Chapter 1

What Should We be Assessing?

Madeleine Atkins

INTRODUCTION

A review of assessment practices in higher education is certainly timely. External and internal factors have combined to highlight many short-comings in the present system and to suggest that the quality of students' learning is being adversely affected by the assessment practices in use (Atkins *et al.*, 1993; Heywood, 1989). These factors include modularization and credit transfer schemes, the rapid expansion in student numbers, and the arrival of NVQs and GNVQs. Concurrently, a growing body of research is confirming the nexus between assessment methods on the one hand and learning styles, strategies and outcomes on the other (see, for example, Marton *et al.*, in Laurillard, 1984; Entwistle and Entwistle, 1991; Entwistle, 1992; Otter, 1992).

But underneath the quite proper professional and technical concerns with improving the way we assess students there lurk some deeper, awkward, questions:

What *should* we be assessing?

What is *distinctively special* about a degree?

What *are* the purposes of higher education?

It is these questions which this chapter begins to address.

So what are the purposes of higher education? I suggest that four can be distinguished at the moment:

1. To provide a general educational experience of intrinsic worth in its own right.

Note: This chapter is based in part on the report *Assessment Issues in Higher Education* commissioned by the Department of Employment. However, the views expressed in this chapter are those of the author herself and not necessarily those of the co-authors of the report or of the Employment Department.

2. To prepare students for knowledge creation, application and dissemination.

3. To prepare students for a specific profession or occupation.

4. To prepare students for general employment.

These purposes are certainly not mutually exclusive; indeed they overlap in interesting ways, and the balance between them may shift at different points in a student's degree programme as well as between programmes and between institutions. Nor will there be agreement as to the value to be attached to the different purposes. It is quite likely that students and employers will value the obviously instrumental purposes more highly than do academic staff (Otter, 1992). But the purposes deserve some scrutiny for the issues they raise about the knowledge, understanding and skills that students should be acquiring. And they pose the uncomfortable question of whether we should be trying to define an undergraduate curricular experience in something more than generic competence terms.

THE GENERAL EDUCATIONAL EXPERIENCE

The provision of a general educational experience of intrinsic worth to the student can be broken down into several sub-components. The following are suggested:

- the development of the 'trained mind', ie, critical thinking and reasoning skills, independence of thought, an ability to think conceptually and to bring an intellectual perspective to bear on issues

- the acquisition of knowledge needed to be an educated person arising from exposure to different domains of knowledge, to different cultures, and to the important contemporary theories in the arts and sciences

- personal development for adult life which values the affective, moral and creative aspects of personality as well as the cognitive, and pays attention to educating the future citizen as well as the future employee

- establishing a base for lifelong learning.

Development of the trained mind

Many academics would argue that the development of the 'trained mind' is central to what they do, and that existing assessment methods such as the essay and the unseen written examination paper are a valid way to test it. Unfortunately, it's an assumption that is rarely challenged. How many departments, for example, routinely analyse the written comments on students' work to see the extent to which lecturers are engaging with the substance of the intellectual argument presented or simply commenting on presentation and format? Yet one could argue that of all the sub-components listed above, the 'trained mind' has the most to offer those who seek a more instrumental role for higher education in the economy and that it deserves more conscious, systematic treatment in designing undergraduate programmes of study, including assessment methods, than it currently receives.

Critical thinking should probably now be taken to include the use of computer-based tools and numerical methods for the testing and elaboration of ideas (MacFarlane Report, 1992). Put another way, higher education should aim to do more than give students basic competences in information technology, useful though these are. Basic competences, such as word-processing and manipulation of databases do not, in any case, seem to be *distinctively* the province of higher education though they are frequently listed as outcomes of undergraduate courses. For a more sophisticated approach to what could be acquired one might consider the following:

- an understanding of how computer-based tools can complement and extend the characteristics of human cognition when creating knowledge or solving complex problems

- an understanding of whether the algorithmic or binary nature of computer-based applications fits well or badly with the characteristics of a particular discipline – its methodologies and tests for truth

- an awareness of current developments in multimedia and telecommunications technologies and their impact on organizational structures and patterns of work

- an understanding of how current definitions of knowledge may be changing in the light of such developments as the Internet.

A further point to make about the 'trained mind' is that we know surprisingly little about how it develops, though diagnostic and formative feedback to students are likely to be crucial (and if modularization means more summative and less formative assessment this may be a counter-productive development). The work of Perry (1970) is often cited in this context. He put forward a stage model of intellectual development based on his work with students at Harvard in the late 1960s. The model links intellectual and moral development in an interesting way, thus addressing several aspects of the general educational purpose of higher education. But it suffers from the rigidity of many stage models. For example, it does not fully allow for the influence of the learning context, the nature of the specific learning task on which the student is engaged, or the form of assessment in use. Yet we know now that these factors exert a profound influence on learning styles and therefore the extent to which critical thinking is called into play.

Not only do we not know how the 'trained mind' develops, we also do not know whether the 'trained mind' is a generic and generalizable characteristic or whether it is discipline-specific. Is a 'trained mind' which results from three years study of engineering rather different from the 'trained mind' which results from three years study of linguistics or economics? And, as a corollary, should we be trying to assess the 'trained mind' just in a subject-specific context or is there a case for testing its acquisition through exercises independent of subject domain? Coming full circle, should there be modules on scientific thought for scientists or (what may seem an old-fashioned idea) should all students be required to take a module in philosophy that introduces them to different types of reasoning and critical enquiry?

Knowledge needed to be an educated person

This sub-component raises some controversial issues too. Is it possible or desirable to define (and assess) an 'educated graduate'? If the dominant ideology is that truths are relative, that no one piece of knowledge is more worthwhile acquiring than any other, and that no one culture has a better claim to be studied than any other, the answer may well be that it is not possible to define, let alone assess, the characteristics of an 'educated graduate'. Further, many people in universities would claim that 'academic freedom' implies the right to determine the content of undergraduate programmes without government interference – though of course the content of many vocational courses is laid down by professional accrediting bodies.

Nevertheless, the argument for defining a knowledge-based general curriculum for higher education could be made, as it has been for the school sector, and it might not be as restrictive as many fear even if the underlying dynamic is instrumental. Take, for example, what is happening in France in the Grandes Ecoles where *la culture generale* is being re-emphasized in their highly vocational management training courses (Parry, 1994). There, the humanities are seen as fundamentally relevant to the competitive world of international business. Core studies (analytical reading and discourse, exploration of contemporary social, economic and political issues, foreign languages) are complemented by cultural electives focusing on the arts – not only to provide personal enrichment but also to give students the opportunity to reflect on the imaginative and aesthetic dimensions of human endeavour so that they can transfer the principles observed to their own sphere of professional activity.

So, should there be compulsory modules on the contemporary world for all students? Should all students acquire some level of useful proficiency in a foreign language? If one distinctive aspect of an institution of higher education is its international outlook, should not module content and assessment reflect this more purposively than at present? This would mean a more fundamental reshaping of the curriculum than simply engaging in ERASMUS, TEMPUS and their successors, or having staff networked through research projects to colleagues in other countries. One can argue that by 2005 our concept of 'internationalization' as a university goal will need to be much more sophisticated than it is now, with concomitant consequences for the professional development of academic staff.

The development of a base for lifelong learning

This raises issues too. There may be more that we need to do under the heading of 'learning to learn' than study skills, however well intentioned. Again, there is a case for students acquiring something more substantive in the way of knowledge about conceptual development, cognitive acceleration, learning styles, etc. It might also be advantageous to introduce them to the current debate about competence, knowledge and understanding, and the way that their interrelationships may define what counts as 'learning' both at university and subsequently or concurrently in their place of employment.

Finally, the notion of a generally educated graduate raises the issue of who is to be responsible for monitoring a student's intellectual development and general knowledge acquisition. The answer usually given is the personal tutor. There is little empirical evidence on what personal tutors currently do. But one suspects that diagnostic assessment of intellectual development, feedback and monitoring is rarely part of it. Anecdotally, at least, students are fortunate if they see their tutor twice a semester, and the agenda for their meetings is likely to be predominantly administrative or welfare in nature rather than academic in the strictest sense.

Preparation for knowledge creation, application and dissemination

One can argue that the characteristics of this purpose include the following:

- acquisition of the conceptual frameworks, major current theories, and basic formulae of the subject studied

- deep and detailed knowledge of some aspects of the subject; development of personal preferences with a view to further specialization

- an understanding of the subject's methodologies and procedures, tests for truth, ethical constraints and ways of handling evidence and argument

- experience, at first vicarious but then first-hand, of knowledge creation through a small-scale project or research study

- insight into how subject knowledge changes, problem solving occurs and into the provisional nature of current understanding

- uses and limitations of models, numerical techniques, etc.

- development of the skills of communication pertinent to the disciplinary culture to which the subject belongs

- development of group or team working skills if appropriate in the discipline.

Of the various sub-categories, it is possible that the third tends to get squeezed out; several may be at risk from the fragmentation of modularization. But understanding how a subject works, how its practitioners go about constructing and testing knowledge, does seem to be a very proper concern of higher education and a useful acquisition for students to take with them when they move into their occupations – even if specific items of subject knowledge become outdated or are simply forgotten.

At a more general level this purpose of higher education does make us face the interesting if uncomfortable debate about specialist knowledge versus transferable skills. There is now some evidence to support the view that as one develops specialist expertise the more one's decision making and information processing strategies are carried out at a 'smart' subconscious level, finely attuned to particular, repeated contexts (Bruner, 1992; English, 1992). So the more expert one becomes, the harder it may be to think, act and solve problems in quite different contexts. Do we want emergent expertise or cognitive flexibility in our graduates? Which should assessment practices reflect?

This dilemma is present too in the concept of the 'knowledge worker' which, we are told, is what graduates are likely to become in the Europe of the twenty-first century. What exactly is a knowledge worker? Is it someone who will add to what is known in increasingly fragmented sub-specialisms, in which case we may need to reassert the importance of graduates knowing something substantive at the end of three years of university life. (And, coincidentally, reform the traditional assessment practices the better to fulfil this aim.) Or is it someone who will synthesize gobbets of information held in global databases and apply it to a whole range of different situations and tasks? In which case a general, multi-disciplinary curriculum, with modules specifically designed to train students to transfer knowledge and skills to new situations, may be the better course to follow.

Preparation for a specific profession or occupation

This purpose can be broken down into the following sub-categories:

- integration of theoretical knowledge with knowledge of processes and principles developed from analysis of practice

- acquisition of expertise derived from subject-specific knowledge and from its application or interpretation in real contexts

- development of skills and competences such as interacting with clients gained through first-hand experience of professional contexts and feedback on performance from skilled practitioners

- acquisition of the norms, attitudes, personal qualities and collegial ways of working expected of members of the target profession

- understanding and demonstration of any ethical codes and procedures expected in the profession

- understanding of the organizational contexts in which one is likely to be working and of the evolving role of the profession in society at large

- ability to reflect on one's own practice, to use feedback to assess and manage one's own performance, and to determine one's own continuing professional development needs.

The last of the sub-categories – commonly termed 'the reflective practitioner' – is seen unquestioningly as a desirable outcome of vocational training. Indeed, current models of novice-expert development suggest that without a considered evaluation of performance it is difficult to move from experience to expertise. But it would be a pity if undue concentration on the reflective practitioner left too little time for knowledge and understanding of how professional practice is constrained, shaped and given meaning by the organizations and cultures in which the professional works; about what happens at the boundary between the professional's immediate sphere of action and the managerial structures of the organization and how that, in turn, may enhance or diminish the effectiveness of that person's work; about professional dilemmas which are insoluble at the level of the individual and the consequent need sometimes for collective action if the individual is not to feel disempowered. So there is a case for saying that graduates need to know something about how organizations are structured and how people in them behave and also about how working practices and individual work patterns are changing as we head into the next century.

Preparation for general employment

The following characteristics can be distinguished here:

- first-hand work experience in a variety of settings
- development of the ability to reflect on and learn from practical experiences
- development of mental competences including numeracy, quick assimilation of large amounts of information and analysis of issues from several perspectives
- development of communication skills including oral presentation and report writing
- development of technical skills including use of generic software, communications technologies and foreign language for business
- development of personal qualities including drive, self-motivation, time management, working without close supervision, leadership, enterprise, initiative
- development of applied skills such as working in a group, problem solving, evaluating risks and consequences
- understanding the nature of change and preparedness to adapt appropriately.

These characteristics are very familiar to those who have been involved in the Enterprise in Higher Education programme or who have followed debates about skill shortages in the economy. There is an underlying assumption, yet to be firmly substantiated, that such competences and skills when acquired in a higher education context are indeed transferred to employment. Perhaps more cynically, many of these characteristics are being endorsed, at least on paper, through the departmental claims of excellence, written in the hope of a Higher Education Funding Council for England quality assessment visit. (Whether the departments actually assess students for these skills and competences, or have designed curricula specifically to develop them, is another matter.)

Clearly, with half of all graduates entering employment on completion of their degree, and with 40 per cent of job vacancies non-specific as to subject studied, higher education has to take this purpose seriously. The issue is whether it has done so in a distinctive and valuable manner, or whether the level at which it is operationalizing these skills and competences could be achieved just as well, and considerably more cheaply, by other agencies. If the latter is true, then the way forward may well be to merge the first and fourth purposes of higher education. This might mean reconceptualizing some aspects of the *general* educational purpose for an employment context, but this should not be a particularly difficult task. As argued earlier, the distinctive outcomes of a degree programme – the trained mind, cultural sensitivity, linguistic competence and an ability to learn – seem eminently marketable qualities for a graduate to possess.

CONCLUSION

In this chapter I have tried to raise some of the issues which face those who are seeking to improve the learning experience of students in higher education. I have argued that those issues are not just to do with teaching methods, assessment techniques and staff training. Inescapably, the issues are about what students should be learning and who is going to define it. And the answers cannot just be in terms of rather low-level generic skills and competences if higher education is to justify its costly existence in the twenty-first century. There also has to be a debate about the knowledge and understanding that one should expect a student to gain from an undergraduate programme, unfashionable though such a debate has been for some time, and difficult though it is within the current NVQ/GNVQ frameworks.

Chapter 2

Assessment and Learning:
Contradictory or Complementary?

David Boud

There is probably more bad practice and ignorance of significant issues in the area of assessment than in any other aspect of higher education. This would not be so bad if it were not for the fact that the effects of bad practice are far more potent than they are for any aspect of teaching. Students can, with difficulty, escape from the effects of poor teaching, they cannot (by definition, if they want to graduate) escape the effects of poor assessment. Assessment acts as a mechanism to control students that is far more pervasive and insidious than most staff would be prepared to acknowledge. It appears to conceal the deficiencies of teaching as much as it does to promote learning. If, as teachers and educational developers, we want to exert maximum leverage over change in higher education, we must confront the ways in which assessment tends to undermine learning.

I have been reinforced in my view of the importance of assessment considerations by the work of my former colleagues in the Professional Development Centre at the University of New South Wales. Sue Toohey teaches the subject on assessment in the postgraduate course for university teachers. At the beginning she asks them to write an auto-biography focusing on their experiences of being assessed. The results of this are devastating and the students cannot stop themselves from referring to it in other classes. They emerge from the exercise saying to themselves that they must not treat their students in the same ways in which they were treated. It is clear from this that even successful, able and committed students – those who become university teachers – have been hurt by their experiences of assessment, time and time again, through school and through higher education. This hurt did not encourage them to persist and overcome adversity as some of our more intellectually muscular colleagues might argue: it caused them to lose confidence, it dented their self-esteem and led them never to have anything to do with some subjects ever again. Now, some of these incidents were connected

35

with abuses of power by teachers and could not be justified on any grounds, but others were artefacts of everyday assessment practices which we regard as perfectly normal. If assessment has such a profound effect on the successes of the system, how much greater must be the negative effects on their less academically accomplished peers?

Interest in assessment in higher education has been at a low point for about a decade and it has only been in the 1990s that it has started to pick up again. I have been surprised, in coming back to it after a long absence, that it is not the measurement-driven and rather stagnant area that I remembered it to be, but it is now at the heart of considerations of teaching and learning. It actually always was at the heart of such matters, but in the hands of assessment specialists it was easy to gain the impression that it required a knowledge of particular statistical techniques and test-construction that didn't have much relationship to acts of learning. The dominant discourse in the literature referred to reliability, validity, discrimination (as a desirable feature, of course!) and difficulty.

That has now changed dramatically. Assessment is back, centre-stage, and is of wide interest and concern. The assessment load created by increasing numbers of students and the shift in thinking towards competency frameworks are but the most prominent of many pressures. This is not to say that discussions of teaching and learning are always central to discussions of assessment, but it does mean that we cannot possibly ignore assessment issues: assessment certainly aids or inhibits our endeavours in improving teaching and learning.

A concept which became part of the assessment discourse and which influenced my earlier thinking was Scriven's (1967) distinction between formative evaluation (to improve) and summative evaluation (to decide). These terms were translated on this side of the Atlantic into formative and summative assessment and used to discuss the importance of making sufficient provision for feedback to students as distinct from marking or grading which did not provide useful information to them. At times, the discussion seemed to imply that it was possible to make a clean separation between the two and that one could provide separate assessment tasks for formative and summative purposes. This did not prove to be a fruitful path as the dominance of summative assessment in the minds of students (and in the practices of staff) was so great that it tended to swamp the more modest endeavours of formative assessment. Now we see that we must consider both aspects together, at all times. Too often assessment is led by the needs of summative judgement, not learning. It is ironic that it doesn't even serve the needs of the former very well.

My discussion starts from the premise that assessment for accreditation or certification cannot be separated from assessment for learning. Assessment always leads to learning. But the fundamental question is, 'what kind of learning?' What do our acts of assessment communicate to students? I hope to show that assessment and learning are in an uneasy state of tension at present but that it is possible to move towards complementarity. The starting point is: what do students learn from assessment? From there assessment is viewed in terms of consequences, the development of thinking about assessment is considered and the important, but neglected, issue of language in assessment is explored.

ASSESSMENT ALWAYS LEADS TO LEARNING. BUT INTENDED OR NOT?

Every act of assessment gives a message to students about what they should be learning and how they should go about it. The message is coded, is not easily understood and often it is read differently and with different emphases by staff and by students. The message is always interpreted in context and the cues which the context provides offer as much or more clues to students than the intentions of staff, which are rarely explicit.

Good assessment is not just a matter of finding the 'appropriate' method and using it sensibly in conjunction with given subject matter. There are always unintended consequences in assessment. Students will learn to adopt surface approaches to study in some circumstances and will adopt deep or strategic approaches in others. In so doing they will be prompted partly by the forms and nature of assessment tasks. They will learn that, in order to maximize their marks, they should use rote learning in many circumstances, even when we might believe that this would distract them from the most important aspects of the course. This response – and other undesirable ones – will not only be a function of the assessment tasks set, but of all the experiences of assessment students have had in the past. (See Kohn, 1993, for example, for a discussion of the negative long-term effects of instrumental approaches to assessment and appraisal.) If, for example, they get the idea that memorization works for multiple-choice tests, then they will persist in that strategy even when reassured that this won't be helpful. Students are not simply responding to the given subject – they carry with them the totality of their experiences of learning and being assessed and this certainly extends far beyond concurrent and immediately preceding subjects.

Assessment is the most significant prompt for learning. One of the most important outcomes of research on student learning is the recognition that learning must fundamentally be seen as relational (Ramsden, 1987). That is, learning is a function of both teaching and the context in which it occurs. It is not a matter of learners engaging with a body of knowledge to which they have been introduced, but of how this is interpreted by them and the actions which they take as a result of these interpretations. Assessment can encourage passive, reproductive forms of learning while simultaneously hiding the inadequate understanding to which such forms of learning inevitably lead (Entwistle and Ramsden, 1983; Ramsden, 1988). This means that in terms of assessment, student approaches to learning are a function of:

●   the intrinsic qualities of the form of assessment being used

●   the ways in which the assessor translates the material to be assessed into the given format and selects assessment tasks appropriate for the subject and the specific learning goals and, most importantly,

●   how the student *interprets* the task at hand and the context of the assessment.

The latter interpretation is not just dependent on the form of the assessment process, but on how these tasks are embedded within the total context of the subject and within the total experience of the course and of university life. The perceptions and interactions of a student are more important to learning than what staff take for granted as the 'reality' of the assessment. These perceptions cannot be assumed: they are only available from the students themselves.

But more is needed. Students experience the interaction effects of one form of assessment on another. In any given month they may have to complete ten assessment tasks, in another month only one. The ways in which they approach each of these will be influenced by the others. A task which is intrinsically interesting and which may be approached meaningfully at any other time may be given short shrift when it is located among a thicket of examinations. Very little attention has been given to the compounding effects of assessment even when we know that it is the total array of demands in a given period which influences how each one is tackled.

THE CRITERION OF CONSEQUENCES

An important concept related to this notion of learning that can help us in our discussions on assessment relates to the consequences of any given act of assessment. It has recently emerged in the USA and was prompted no doubt by the rise of interest in the philosophy and ethics of con-sequentialism (Pettit, 1993). *Consequential validity* refers to the effect of the test or other form of assessment on learning and other educational matters (Linn *et al.*, 1991; Messick, 1989). It prompts the question, 'What are the broader consequences of a given assessment activity beyond those which are immediately evident?' Consequential validity is high when there is a positive backwash effect on learning and low when it encourages ways of learning which are counter to what is desired. It points to links between learning and assessment; it is not just another new self-referential test statistic. We should develop assessment procedures of high consequential validity which, for example, encourage students to adopt good study approaches, learning what it is most desirable for them to learn.

There is growing interest in exploring the dimension of consequences. While they have not been directly using the conception I have just introduced, Graham Gibbs and his colleagues at the Oxford Centre for Staff Development have been promoting the use of action research to develop deep approaches to learning (Gibbs, in press). A vital part of this work is finding out what it is that students actually do. We need to know what approaches to learning students are adopting, what students' expectations are of different assessment tasks and what they choose to do and what they choose not to do in response to the different assessment regimes which are introduced. There is no substitute for knowing our students' learning practices well enough to be able to intervene in helpful ways. This is not just a principle of good assessment but is, of course, fundamental to our role in fostering learning.

Encouraging deep approaches to learning is one aspect we might explore in considering consequences. Another is the impact which assessment has on the capacities and skills students have in being able to assess themselves. This is of greater long-term significance than the effect of any specific subject-matter learning. Students must leave university equipped to engage in self-assessment throughout their professional lives. They need to be able to make reliable judgements about what they do and do not know and what they can and cannot do. Too often staff-driven assessment encourages students to be dependent on the teacher or the examiners to make decisions about what they know and they do not effectively learn to be able to do this for themselves. Well-designed assessment practices should be oriented around the key concepts and ideas that students should be able to deal with, but the devastating phenomenographic research on concept acquisition in first-year classes (for example, Dahlgren, 1984) shows that courses tend neither to develop basic concepts well, nor use assessment tasks which allow staff *or students* to know whether concepts have been learned.

At present, students learn most about self-assessment through their own informal second-guessing of their performance on the assessment tasks which are set but this is rarely adequate. Even the most able, cue-seeking students (Miller and Parlett, 1974) would find it difficult to discern, and to work out how to apply, the criteria implicit in much of the assessment to which they are subject. We need to find a variety of ways of giving practice to students in self-assessment. In particular we need to develop those self-assessment activities in which they, and staff, are required to engage with the criteria which distinguish acceptable from unacceptable performance and to actively encourage, rather than discourage self-assessment – as traditional assessment does (Boud, 1991).

DEVELOPMENTS IN ASSESSMENT THINKING

In considering changing views of assessment, I have found it useful to think of the evolution of our ideas in terms of a number of stages of development (see Eisner, 1993, for a different formulation emphasizing US developments). Each stage emerged during a particular period of time and within each there were particular preoccupations among those discussing assessment. In present-day discussions we can see concerns of each stage appearing and being influential. While each arose as a result of particular concerns at the time, we presently exist with the conceptions from different eras being held simultaneously in any given institution – often side-by-side in staff in the same course. I want to outline these stages to lead to what I believe to be an emergent conception of assessment which is qualitatively different from those generally held now in higher education.

Conventional assessment

It was taken for granted that assessment *follows* teaching and that the aim of assessment is to discover how much has been learned. Learning was viewed quantitatively in terms of the amount of the teaching which had been absorbed. There was little interest in the specifics of which questions had been 'correctly' answered and the unseen examination – the most favoured method – frequently allowed for some choice. Conventional assessment closely follows traditional patterns of assessment practices in a given discipline area: there are differences between assessment practices in different fields of knowledge, but this is not normally a matter of general interest.

While other forms of assessment, particular those which are used in continuous assessment – for example, reports, essays and short tests – now form part of the conventional pattern and have been absorbed in the conventional conception, there has not been any overall raising of the awareness of levels of sophistication among staff about assessment to

accompany this. The adding of marks or scores which are incommen-
surable is a common and unquestioned practice.

Educational measurement

Educational measurement takes for granted the basic assumptions of
conventional assessment: that is, testing follows teaching, the links
between subject content and assessment technique are unproblematic
and assessment is quantitative. The main concerns of educational
measurement are to make assessment more rational, efficient and tech-
nically defensible. Ideas drawn from the field of psychometrics are part of
the vocabulary.

Although measurement concepts have mainly affected external public
examinations, many of which have now become quite psychometrically
sophisticated, the influences have crept into higher education along with
methods such as multiple-choice testing which is the only method from
this stage of assessment thinking which has had a significant impact. The
use of multiple choice tests brought to the fore considerations of reliability and validity and the formal notion of question difficulty.

Competency and authentic assessment

Concerns about validity heralded the new era which we have now
entered. Was there correspondence between what was assessed and what
students were expected to do after they had graduated? Are existing tests
the best vehicles for determining whether students have an appropriate
understanding or can perform at a suitable standard? More radical
concerns were raised about whether assessment revealed any useful
information about what a given student could actually do and whether
assessment had a negative backwash effect on learning. The earliest signs
of the new era were small shifts away from norm-referenced towards
criterion-referenced assessment. Criterion-referenced or mastery tests in
themselves are not adequate because the problems are often contrived
and the cues are artificial. They can unwittingly reinforce the idea that
mere right answers put forth by going through the motions are adequate
signs of achievement. What are required are authentic assessments:
'contextualised complex intellectual challenges, not fragmented and
static bits or tasks' (Wiggins, 1989, p. 711).

Some implications from new thinking about competency are starting to
have an impact, although not in the obvious way. It is not the competency
movement which focuses on lower-level vocational skills and potentially
reductionistic formulations of objectives which is significant, but the
moves by professional bodies to ensure that there is closer correspon-

dence between higher education courses and professional practice (Gonczi, 1994). It is the notion that what is important are learning outcomes, no matter how they were achieved and the specification of assessment tasks which indicate outcomes independent of the preparation for them. And it is the use of more naturalistic *in situ*, multifaceted, forms of assessment which provides the new challenge.

In higher education it does not necessarily mean a shift to more external forms of assessment – indeed it might not mean this at all – but it will mean that the cosy and unquestioned relationship between a course and the assessment 'which forms part of it' will be open to critical scrutiny from an outcomes-oriented perspective. The positive aspect is that assessment will be related to outcomes in a discipline or field of practice which can be publicly justified – to colleagues, to students and to external bodies. The potentially negative aspect is teaching for the test, but this should not be as bad as it once was if the test is authentic and well-constructed.

TOWARDS AN HOLISTIC VIEW OF ASSESSMENT

Whatever the claimed motives of assessment in the first two conceptions above, the *de facto* priority was forms of assessment which compared individuals with each other rather than engaged in assessment with respect to criteria or notions of competence. The issue of the links between competence, learning and assessment have now come to prominence. Good assessment now is that which both closely reflects desired learning outcomes and in which the process of assessment has a directly beneficial influence on the learning process.

This is a major challenge for all staff. They will need to become far less the test-setter thinking of items to test knowledge acquisition or the marker processing large numbers of examination scripts. They will need to become researchers of students' perceptions, designers of multi-faceted assessment strategies, managers of assessment processes and consultants assisting students in the interpretation of rich information about their learning. There will have to be less assessment for staff to process if they are to have time to make these qualitative changes. But, this will need to be done so that there will not be fewer opportunities for students to practise and gain feedback. Here is another important role for self- and peer-assessment.

We are now seeing moves to a holistic conception: no longer can we think of assessment merely as the sum of its parts, all of which can be considered separately, or make a distinction between the work as a whole and particular aspects of it (see, for example, Hager *et al.*, 1994). We need to look at the impact of the total package of learning and assessment and not simply at fragments of assessment. This means that we must inevitably look at the profile of assessment *as students see it*, from the point of view of the course, the total experience of the whole. The move to modularized courses which operate as a smorgasbord makes this task much more difficult, but it is a challenge which must be faced.

The discussion so far has been posited on traditional power relationships between student and teacher/assessor, but in an holistic conception this assumption must also be challenged. The very act of a person or authority making unilateral and final judgements over another has major consequences for learning. If students are to become autonomous and interdependent learners as argued in statements of aims of higher education (for example, see Boud, 1988a), then the relationship between student and assessor must be critically examined and the limiting influences of such an exercise of power explored. The new agenda for assessment research needs to place this as a high priority if we are not to be distracted, as has so often occurred in the past, by technicalities.

THE LANGUAGE OF ASSESSMENT

The final issue to be considered relates to the whole of assessment and it is particularly important because it concerns an aspect of our practice in all aspects of education which is all-pervasive but invisible most of the time. Earlier, I drew attention to the importance of student perceptions of assessment and the interaction of students with learning and assessment, but there is an additional aspect. It is a key factor in a lot of the hurt that we have all experienced in our careers as assessees. It is the effect of the language we use in talking about and making assessments.

Not surprisingly, in an act which involves judgement, we use judgemental language. Ironically, it is this which creates much of the difficulty. We judge too much and too powerfully, not realizing the extent to which students experience our power over them. Learning is an act which necessarily leaves us vulnerable: we open ourselves to changes in the ways we see the world, not knowing where we shall end up. We might find a secure spot or be exposed. Rarely are we confident about what we know during the early stages (which include most of the time we are being taught) – the very stages at which we are mostly likely to receive the comments from a teacher. We know how little we know and we fear the depths of our ignorance. To have someone come along and tell us that, for example, what we are doing is all wrong or that we will never do it well or that we haven't read the book when we thought we had, is a direct attack on us when we are least able to cope with it. In treating students in such ways, and, indeed, with some students by using far less direct forms, we go beyond the realm of valid statements into the world of abusive language. It abuses them in the sense of taking undue advantage of them by virtue of our position, of betraying them. It does not seem abusive to us, but to those on the receiving end, it is profoundly so.

Too often we fail to make absolutely clear the distinction between giving feedback on a specific product which has been produced by a person and judging them as a person. We write and say things which can readily be taken as comments about the person rather than their work and in doing so we link in to the doubts and uncertainties which they have of themselves and our remarks are magnified at great cost to the self-esteem of the persons concerned.

We have to be especially careful about using what Rorty terms 'final vocabulary'. This is the use of vocabulary which uses terms such as 'good', 'right', 'rigorous', 'professional standards' and the like (Rorty, 1989, p. 73). Even though it is apparently positive, it is language which leaves no room for manoeuvre. It has the final say. It classifies without recourse to reconsideration or further data, and it does not allow for other possibilities. Not only are terms such as these – even more so in the negative or implied negative versions – damaging, but they communicate nothing of substance. They are empty rhetoric, more at home in the editorial posturing of the conservative press than in any discourse about learning.

I suspect we use them because they come easily to hand; they help us avoid having to engage with the substance of what we are commenting on and they give the impression that we are concerned with quality and standards without anything of quality being said. We must break any bad habits we might have acquired and choose our words carefully with an eye to the consequences. If we do this, then we can provide something valuable which learners can use to change what they do, and not have to worry about defending themselves from the (hopefully) inadvertent use of words which oppress. We need to avoid the simplistic response of cleaning up our terminology while retaining the same universalist sentiments. It is missing the point to steer away from obvious final vocabulary through rephrasing comments into more 'correct' forms. The form betrays the intention; it is the intention which must be changed.

One way to begin to address this problem is to stick with descriptive feedback which conveys in detail what, from our explicitly *subjective* point of view, is and is not manifest in the work, rather than expressed as a statement by some apparently absolute authority about what the learner can and cannot do. We need not only to avoid the negative global and abstract words of judgement, but the positive as well, for implied negatives are always close at hand and learners do read the comments on other people's work. Grades are a form of 'final vocabulary' and if they cannot be avoided they must be directly linked with rich statements of competence which meaningfully elaborate on what the grade purports to summarize.

Another important way of avoiding final statements is to shift away from the practice of assessment which occurs only at the end of a period of study or which does not allow for the possibility of response. If dialogue between staff and students is a normal part of assessment practices, there is often a human incentive to avoid the grosser forms of final vocabulary and other dismissive language and there is the opportunity for rich and detailed information to be exchanged that is helpful for both parties. The use of negotiated profiles of achievement also has potential value here. Where they provide specific, descriptive information on achievements they are worthwhile but when they read like a collection of unsolicited testimonials – the home of final vocabulary – they will be of use to no one.

There are, of course, forms of oppression in teaching and assessment which inappropriately and offensively discriminate between individuals or groups in ways which are anathema to academic purposes and which directly act to inhibit the achievements of students. This is a matter of great importance which needs to be explored further in the assessment context, but a useful starting point is to examine the differential use of the types of language which I have just mentioned. I am not referring here just to obviously offensive racist remarks, the apparent invisibility of certain group members or the issue of gender-inclusive language – these are some of very many important aspects of this issue – but the use also of illustrations and examples which favour members of dominant groups, materials used in culturally insensitive ways and assumptions made about learners on little more than their appearance or apparent background. These are matters which deserve far greater attention in all aspects of academic work as the evidence of the deleterious effect of such matters on learning is building rapidly (see, for example, Hayes and Colin, 1994; Luke and Gore, 1992; Pettman, 1991; Thomas, 1990).

TAKING THE DISCUSSION FURTHER

The issues raised here are not ones that allow for ready solutions, but they are matters with which staff in higher education need to engage if improvements in the quality of assessment and student learning are to be made. To assist in the process of further discussion the accompanying checklist aims to provide a prompt for the consideration of assessment issues in the context of a particular course. In a few cases items which go beyond the earlier discussion have been included to balance the list and items which are commonly discussed in assessment texts have been omitted.

How should we judge assessment? Questions to prompt critical reflection

1. Focus and interpretation of assessment

- Are assessment tasks oriented towards the world external to the course, that is to say are they not simply self-referential?

- How are they related to the central outcomes desired as part of education for a given discipline, field or profession?

- Are assessment tasks interpreted by students in the ways assumed by staff, that is to say, do both parties have the same perceptions about the capabilities to be exercised and ideas and concepts to be engaged?

2. Contribution of assessment to overall learning goals

- In assessment tasks are learners commonly required to engage in the whole of a process or only in fragments (for example, problem-formulation as well as problem-solving)?

- Is as much emphasis to be given to the strategy and process of what is required as to the specific result?

- Can each separate act of assessment in itself be credibly regarded as a worthwhile contribution to learning?

- Does the totality of assessment tasks across subjects adequately portray what is most important for learning in the course?

3. Consequences of assessment

- What are the actual consequences (intended and unintended) of any given act of assessment: on student learning, on teaching, on the curriculum?

- What are the consequences of the total diet of assessment experienced by any given student: on the student, on staff, on the course?

- In particular, does assessment act to encourage quality learning throughout a course (for example, deep/meaningful approaches to study) and discourage undesired learning practices (short-term memorizing for tests)?

4. Contribution of assessment to lifelong learning development

- Does the range of assessment tasks leave students better equipped to engage in their own self-assessment now and in the future?

- Is the development of student autonomy necessarily encouraged through an overall assessment strategy for a course which takes account of the demands of each subject?

- Are students able to avail themselves of sufficient opportunities to shape assessment tasks and requirements (including assessment criteria) to meet their own needs and interests (for example, through negotiating specific assessment tasks)?

5. Appropriate language and assumptions of assessment

- Is 'final vocabulary' avoided in statements of assessment (for example, is feedback about particular task-related accomplishments emphasized and abstract judgemental vocabulary excluded at all times)?

- Do assessment activities make assumptions about the subject matter or the learner which are *irrelevant* to the task and which are differentially perceived by different groups of students (for example, use of unnecessarily gender-specific examples, assumptions about characteristics, etc.)?

6. Portrayal of accomplishments

- Does assessment lead to the production of a profile or other form of documentation which fully and fairly portrays the accomplishments of a student and which is prepared in collaboration with the person involved?

- Are such accomplishments sufficiently contextualized to enable readers to draw meaningful conclusions from them?

7. Monitoring assessment and promoting good practice

- Is assessment-related work a productive use of time for all those involved (for example, is student and staff learning leading to more effective practice in the future)?

- Are all staff confident in their understanding and skilled in implementing assessment which takes account of the issues considered above?

- Are there assessment guidelines or policies agreed by staff which address the kinds of issues discussed here?

- Are assessment practices and their effects given as much attention in staff discussions and formal review processes as content and staffing matters?

Acknowledgments

I wish to thank Lee Shulman for drawing my attention to the idea of consequential validity and to Angela Brew, Kate Day, Paul Hager and Ranald MacDonald for helpful comments on an earlier version of this chapter.

Chapter 3

Attending to Assessment: A Process for Faculty

T. Dary Erwin

Faculty in the USA share with their colleagues in the UK and the rest of the world a growing need to explain and to document the value of the undergraduate student experience at their respective institutions. Competing budget priorities and questions about quality have produced level funding or even financial cuts. Government officials at all levels as well as the public are increasingly questioning the educational system and how much student learning is being achieved. Some of the major criticisms include:

● students do not have the basic skills of reading, writing, and mathematics to function effectively in the work force and in a competitive society

● there is little consensus about the general education or the knowledge, skills and personal experiences every student should have, regardless of his or her major subject of study, and

● credible measures of student learning are generally not available, particularly at an institutional level.

In the USA, for example, a push for accountability in higher education is coming from centralized government sources. Three National Education Goals for college students were formulated by the President and state governors in 1990. These goals of critical thinking, problem solving and communication skills are to be assessed eventually and are intended to increase global competitiveness (National Center for Education Statistics, 1992). In addition, the procedures for accreditation – or external review of American institutions – are also under attack for lack of rigour and lack of quality assurance. A new federal governmental process, called the State

Note: In the USA the word 'faculty' means academic staff: professors, lecturers and university educators in general.

49

Postsecondary Review Entity (SPRE), is rapidly replacing accreditation commissions which have hitherto monitored and maintained quality at colleges and universities. Unfortunately, without much input from faculty, SPRE definitions of quality pertain to outputs such as graduation and retention rates rather than to the outcomes of education. Over-reliance on simplistic measures of outputs which have little to do with what is happening in the classroom is potentially a problem with such external interventions. This greater scrutiny of higher education is sup-ported by the public, especially by parents who desire harder evidence of institutional effectiveness rather than simply relying on the reputations of institutions. Faculty can no longer view these calls for accountability as a fad but have to see them as a call for academic staff in higher education to give an account of the benefits of their work and of their programmes. Terenzini (1993) explains how faculty in the USA, UK and the European Union are grappling in a similar fashion with the often conflicting pur-poses, methods and processes of assessment.

There are more intrinsic reasons, closer to the day-to-day life of faculty, for incorporating sound assessment practices. What influences or guides faculty when decisions are made about individual students or pro-grammes? Typically, our decisions are based on tradition (it has always been done this way), on logic (it makes sense), on intuition (an inner feeling, perhaps gathered from limited conversations), on politics (non-educational influences), or on information about the effectiveness of our current practices. The assessment of student learning should be provid-ing information that is used, at least in part, to guide faculty decisions about teaching and the curriculum. Assessment should not be the only influence on these decisions, which will also represent the interplay of various values and the availability of resources, and most decisions will be arrived at through the interaction of all of these influences.

A challenge for faculty now is to create innovative assessment methods that are both credible and defensible and to use the information they provide in educational decision making. Stated another way, the assess-ment process really mirrors the academic way: that is, we formulate our hypothesis, gather information about that hypothesis, and revise our hypothesis based on this information. The assessment process then is not a foreign process but engrained in our own training. Unfortunately, grade inflation, awarding grades based on effort and not performance, uneven standards among instructors or among institutions, and a lack of understanding or agreement about education itself have led to the lack of credible measures. A major priority is to develop better assessment practices in order to answer questions such as whether what was thought to be effective is really effective and whether what we intend to happen is really happening with students' learning. It is also a matter of common sense and good ethics to be able to back up our practice with evidence such as that provided by valid and reliable assessment procedures.

This chapter addresses a sequential process of assessment for faculty, namely, what should be assessed, how these objectives should be assessed, and what analytical strategies should be employed on assessment information.

WHAT SHOULD BE ASSESSED?

Deciding what to teach and assess is one issue, not two. In both cases, we are asking what, educationally, it is that we are trying to accomplish. Is it an imparting of knowledge, teaching a skill, instilling a thinking process or way to approach problems, or nurturing a personal trait or characteristic? Knowledge and skill development are traditionally accepted, but assessment has also helped reveal the need for higher order models of cognitive and affective development (Erwin, 1991) if we are to go beyond programmes that are solely concerned with the acquisition of knowledge and the development of often low-level skills.

As one example adopted from Perry's scheme (Erwin, 1983), consider the intellectual development stages of dualism, relativism, commitment and empathy. Dualistic people tend to view the world in dichotomies of either right/wrong, yes/ no, as something to be agreed with immediately or rejected if not familiar to that person. In the next higher stage, relativistic people recognize alternatives but cannot resolve conflicting points of view. Committed people reason about these alternatives and commit themselves to a belief with judgement. In the highest stage, empathetic people make commitments with a sensitivity to the impact of these choices on other people and society. These stages of cognitive complexity or levels of critical thinking have been conceived as stand-alone purposes of education, as general, transferable educational goals. Yet they can profitably be applied to decision making about programmes within disciplines too. For example, dualistic objectives pertain to the vocabulary of the discipline and to the introductory principles and themes. Relativistic thinkers see beyond the facts and begin to compare the themes and principles. The committed person adopts beliefs after reasoning about these alternatives, while the empathetic person evaluates the effects of these commitments on society and other people. Our challenge is to ensure that our teaching does not focus just at the lower levels but also the higher thinking skills in students, which implies that these skills are assessed, not simply written into planning documents.

Such conceptual schemes encompass both thinking and feeling aspects such as flexibility, tolerance of newness, interpersonal relations, multiculturism, and character development. Many faculty accept the difficult challenge of promoting these cognitive and affective developmental aspects because they recognize the value to be had through the development of a lifelong commitment to the higher levels of this scheme. In a survey of 37 major corporations and 36 small firms in the UK, Otter (1992) identified these learning goals as important for graduation:

> access and select information, synthesize and interpret information, demonstrate commitment, demonstrate self discipline, manage personal stress, communicate clearly and accurately, communicate effectively orally, work cooperatively, work alone, accept criticism, understand own strengths and weaknesses, act ethically, and possess basic computer skills (p. 115).

Although another list of Otter's details subject-specific objectives, the above list illustrates (1) the importance of general education or common objectives for all students regardless of major and (2) the importance of personal development characteristics, not just skills or knowledge. The ability to commit oneself through reasoned beliefs and action, the ability to work cooperatively, work independently, accept criticism, manage personal stress, and demonstrate self-discipline, all illustrate an holistic approach to collegiate education. For some faculty, these intended outcomes are difficult to teach, assess and even define. However, their importance in society suggests that faculty do need to take into consideration the teaching and assessment of these broader aspects of education.

Whatever objectives and purposes one has, they must be defined in a specific manner before they are taught or an assessment method can be chosen or designed to measure them. Often, the lack of clarity in objectives, competences, or whatever term one wishes to use, causes confusion about what is in the curriculum and with readers of these objectives. For example, 'students will be able to appreciate, understand, and be familiar with the principles and theories of the discipline'. What do 'appreciate', 'understand', or 'be familiar with' really mean? What are the major principles of the discipline? Does 'familiar' mean recite the major principles or something deeper? What is one trying to achieve with 'appreciate'? These educational objectives are the foundation of a programme or course, and assessment methods should be based on these objectives. Given the need to make them explicit and to share them with students, colleagues, employers and other consumers, there will need to be extensive faculty discussions about them, and these discussions are usually lively, occasionally contentious and controversial, but always positive in establishing the basis for the curriculum and assessment methods.

ASSESSMENT METHODS

Besides the issues of public policy and the need to be clearer about our educational goals, the calls for accountability also point to the need for greater attention to our methods of evaluating instructional and educational experiences. One of the best ways to improve teaching is through better testing. The balance between reliability and validity is discussed by Brown and Knight (1994), yet both reliability and validity are vital for effective information about student learning and development. Just the mere collection of information does not mean this information is of sufficient value to use in our decisions about curriculum and students: the quality of the information is vital. In fact, our past measures of quality are also being questioned, for too often they have appeared to be reliable without being particularly valid, to have measured that which was easily measured, rather than that which was educationally valuable. This section will focus on the most popular of faculty markings, the rating scale.

Essentially, two broad classes of assessment formats may be utilized: selective response and constructed response formats (Bennett and Ward, 1993; Roid and Haladyna, 1982). In a selective response or recognition format, the student chooses among available alternatives, as with multiple-choice questions. Numerous sources exist for writing selective response items (eg, Ebel and Frisbie, 1986; Osterlind, 1989; Wesman, 1972), and their design will not be covered here. In a constructed response format, the student produces a product such as a case study report or lab study, engages in a process or performance such as a social work interview or a musical performance, or exhibits a personal trait such as some leadership ability. Gibbs *et al.*, (1988) provide other examples of active assessment tasks or stimuli. The popularity of more active or performance-based stimuli suggests that more attention be paid to constructed response formats such as a rating scale. For instance, portfolios are widely touted for assessing student learning with student products, processes, performances, or personal traits. However, if portfolios are used, faculty should consider:

- What is the purpose of the assessment?
- What will be in the portfolio?
- How will the student's work in the portfolio be evaluated?

An item of a behaviourally anchored rating scale will be presented below as an illustration of a constructed response format. As the name implies, a behaviourally anchored rating scale contains a series of alternative behaviours from poor to superior descriptions of the concept or task.

Each level of behaviours in the series presents a progressively higher gradient or degree of performance of the product, process, or trait. The rater then chooses the appropriate qualitative level. As a result, we have a clear account of different levels of performance that can be shared with students, so that they have an idea of the criteria against which their work will be graded and which also makes for greater reliability when faculty come to grade the work.

In the following example, students were observed in a small group setting, and one of several aspects of interpersonal communication skills of leadership was to be rated by faculty.

As a leader:

1. Leads conversations, listens well, willing to assume responsibility, keeps check on the direction the meeting is headed, resolves differences by negotiation and shows planning and organization of topic.

2. Able to lead conversations but shows some unwillingness to assume major responsibilities. Some problems with being able to resolve conflicts within the group. Planning and organization needs improvement.

3. Shows lack of flexibility. Runs group without allowing opinion of all to be expressed. Hinders group productivity.

4. Needs more structure while leading group. As a rule, is non-directive to the point that the group is not able to come to needed decisions.

As one item from a multi-item rating scale covering such areas as interviewing style, confidence, organizational skills and other components, this behaviourally anchored rating item lists four alternative sets of behaviours for the leadership area. After observing the student in a small group setting, the rater then chooses the appropriate alternative of 1, 2, 3 or 4. Other areas would be rated similarly. Some persons prefer one 'holistic' rating per student, but multiple ratings over several sub-areas are more diagnostic for the student and for the programme under study. In a behaviourally anchored rating scale, choices typically vary from three to five categories with maximum reliability reached at seven categories or gradients.

When faculty rate a product, process, performance, or personal trait, the rating process introduces measurement error into the final rating. The behaviourally anchored descriptors remove some of this error or uncertainty. However, it is wise to have multiple raters of the same product, process, performance, or personal trait, and calculate an index of agreement. This is often called an inter rater reliability or generalizability coefficient. Low inter-rater reliability or agreement often reflects a lack of focus or uncertainty about what is being measured or what should be taught. This reminds us that it is essential for there to be collaboration among colleagues in order to decide what the programme or course is intended to do and to arrive at shared meanings that can, in turn, be shared with the learners. The issue of reliability is only part of a broader concern about the quality of assessment methods. In the USA, increased governance of higher education by the federal government and by the states is due in part to lack of credibility of the current assessment methods. Improving the validity, and therefore credibility, of our assessment and teaching methods can be undertaken by faculty to reclaim our legacy as certifiers of competence. A brief explanation of validity follows.

Validity is a complex concept which addresses the worth of the assessment for making judgements about students. A more precise definition would state that validity is a judgement about the 'adequacy and appropriateness of inferences and actions' (Messick, 1989, p. 13). Note that an assessment method is not, of itself, valid or otherwise. Conclusions about the validity of a method depend on the inferences we wish to draw from the data it supplies or on the actions we wish to take. As has been explained earlier, our actions are here being expanded beyond the use for a single student to the value and merits of the programme itself. This change in focus from feedback about individuals to accountability of the programme is often referred to as 'high stakes testing'. It follows that the broader the interested audiences, the greater is the need to be confident about the quality of the data themselves in respect of the purpose to which they are being put.

Validity allows us to conceptualize the fitness for purpose of the data we collect and hence to think about ways of improving their quality. Messick (1989, p. 16) observes that some typical questions about validity include:

- Does the content of the assessment method adequately match the content and objectives of the instructional program?

- Is the student responding and reacting to our assessment methods and enquiries in expected ways?

- Does the assessment evidence relate in an expected way to external behaviors?

- Does the assessment method allow us to investigate student differences due to various educational interventions?

- Is the assessment evidence sensitive to the social consequences regarding its use?

These points might be considered when educators are constructing assessment methods. Of course, the more extensive the likely impact of one's inferences from assessment data, the more evidence should be collected for the possible defence of both methods and inferences. It is important to use multiple methods and sources of evidence to present a fuller picture of student learning and development. (See Messick, 1989, for a fuller discussion of validity and Erwin, 1991, for more coverage of rating scales and other assessment methods such as checklists and surveys.)

ANALYTICAL STRATEGIES FOR ANALYSING ASSESSMENT INFORMATION

Assessment studies are not strict experimental studies which yield conclusions about the causal relationship between the educational intervention (the teaching) and the outcome (as revealed by the assessment system). There are several intervening factors such as personal events in a student's life that may influence the outcomes of students' learning. However, an accumulation of evidence from several perspectives or sources can build the case for programme effectiveness, which I have suggested we need to make in a robust manner. Below, four analytical strategies or questions are posed for studying the impact of courses or programmes on students. These questions are: how many students achieve expected minimum competency? Do students who have had the course(s) or educational experience perform better than students who have not had the courses? Are student marks and grades related to or correlated with later outcomes? And do students change over time more than can be explained by the natural process of maturation? Faculty will probably use a combination of these analytical strategies. These analytical strategies will be elaborated below.

How many students achieve *expected competency* in a given programme? Or, stated another way, how many students reach your academic standard or expectations after programme completion? Before information is collected, faculty need to specify the expected score or level of attainment one would expect students to achieve after completion of the programme or unit. Of the students who completed the course or participated in the educational experience, what proportion successfully achieve competency? What differences are there between students who pass and those who do not pass? Ways for determining the standard for minimum competency may be found in Berk (1986) and Erwin (1991).

In a second analytical strategy, we ask whether students who have had the course(s) perform better than students who have not had the courses, experiences, or services. At the most basic level, do students who attended the lectures or participated in the educational experience programme have higher outcomes than students who did not attend or participate? The assessment method should *differentiate between groups* of students who did or did not have the programme or service. For example, if supplemental instructional software is used, do these students learn more? If students participate in an internship in a museum or a business, do they perform better? If students participate and hold leadership positions in organized, out-of-class activities or community groups, do they have better speaking, interpersonal, organization skills, or show higher levels of moral development? Logic would suggest that students who participated fully in the experiences would perform better than students who did not, but information often reveals no difference. If the finding is one of no difference, responses need to be studied to try to see why this is so.

Although it is often difficult to develop sound assessment methods, it is perhaps more difficult to determine why some students learn more than other students. Besides the traditional mode of lecture-style presentation, other instructional modes of delivery offer promise. Active learning approaches give students more responsibility for their learning (Brown and Pendlebury, 1992). Internships, study abroad experiences, interdisciplinary approaches, technology, and student life programmes are popular supplements or alternatives to traditional modes of learning. Multimedia presentations, for instance, must be studied to determine their impact on student learning. On the other hand, some groups of students may be compared with no expectation of any differences. For example, The College of William and Mary unexpectedly found that men out-scored women on an historical knowledge test. Closer examination found more emphasis in history on war and the military, with which men traditionally are more familiar, than was intended. Assessment data can help us to see, then, whether our programmes are indeed fair, or whether there are subtle effects at work that advantage one group of students rather than another in circumstances where no differences would have been predicted.

In the third analytical strategy we ask whether student marks and grades are *related to or correlated with later outcomes*? Depending on one's educational system, a variety of intermediate measures are or can often be collected throughout a student's programme of study. These measures should be related to the student's overall achievement in the programme, which is usually measured at the end of the programme. If course grades or other measures of progress are not related to the intended outcomes of the degree or unit, then closer review of the measures and instruction is needed by the faculty.

A fourth analytical strategy presented here concerns the *change over time* (PCFC/CNAA, 1990). Students should exhibit positive gains over time in some educational objectives. For example, students should increase their critical analysis skills, gain greater independence, and improve their writing skills over the period of their undergraduate experience. It may be a good strategy to assess students on measures of general education as they enter an institution and then to reassess them at graduation.

CONCLUSION

This chapter has summarized a process for assessment ranging from specification of purposes to design of methods and thence to analysing the information. Faculty will probably utilize a combination of these analytical strategies. Whatever objectives, methods, or analytical approaches are adopted, the key is the *use* of the information. Does the information lead to some action? It is very frustrating for faculty to collect information and only then wonder what it means. Ideally, faculty will teach and assess learning with questions that they want to answer, such as how a new instructional technique would work out. The assumption, of course, exists that faculty wish to know about the effectiveness of their courses and programmes through information about quality. Equally, the position is that they *should* wish to know this.

The current focus for many faculty is on the major programme or on general education. In the future, assessment studies of smaller scope will be needed. For example, with advances in technology, faculty will want to know how multimedia approaches and other computer-based systems will affect student learning. Our charge in the future will be to handle more students and to teach just as effectively with diminishing resources due to increased pressure from funding agencies. We must find out what works well and what does not. For example, is the current length of undergraduate programmes optimum? Moreover, educators must also test the effectiveness of new instructional aids before adopting them: can we teach more students just as effectively with multimedia presentations as we could teach fewer students in a traditional lecture-style classroom?

From this perspective there are no negative outcomes for faculty because teaching and student learning are conceived as a continuous process of improvement. Collecting information about the impact of educational programmes and services allows for on-going adjustments with faculty being in an ideal position to serve as evaluators of learning and development. Through processes of assessment, faculty can better explain to themselves and to others the purposes and impact of education. This role of certifying and studying effectiveness is an on-going requirement for faculty. To ignore the calls for accountability is to encourage people external to higher education to establish their own standards rather than ours. Our response is more critical now than ever. And the credibility of our response depends to a large degree on the adequacy of the assessment process we have in place.

Chapter 4

What has Assessment Done for Us – and to Us?

Phil Race

HOW PEOPLE REALLY LEARN

I began the opening session of the conference by telling delegates about a practical model of learning I have been developing on the basis of the replies I gather from a wide range of people on how they learn best (for details see Race, 1994a). The key factors that emerge are:

- the importance of 'the want to learn', or motivation

- the fact that most learning is 'by doing', including practice, and trial and error

- the importance of receiving feedback from other people

- the need to make sense of what has been learned, or to 'digest' it.

I have argued that the 'wanting, doing, feedback, digesting' processes are best thought of in an overlapping way, rather than as a cycle of consecutive steps. I have also discussed elsewhere (Race, 1994b) the conflicts between 'wanting, doing, feedback, digesting' and assessment – particularly thinking of exams. This model can be summed up visually as Figure 4.1.

NIGHTMARES ABOUT ASSESSMENT

One of the most useful ways to identify how to make something better is to think about it at its worst – in other words, 'nightmares'. I asked the conference delegates to close their eyes for a minute, and let their worst fears about assessment come to the surface of their minds. It turned out to be highly productive asking the conference delegates to share the main details of their personal nightmares about assessment. By far the

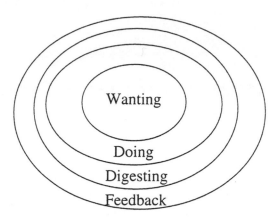

Figure 4.1   *A model of the key processes needed for successful learning*

majority of them thought of exams they had sat, or about nightmares concerning what may have gone wrong with such exams. It should be remembered that generating the detail summarized below took only a minute or two – which shows how readily such details came to the minds of delegates! The details of the nightmares cast grave doubt on the usefulness of exams as a productive stage in the learning experience of students. A few delegates gave details of nightmares about assessing. In this chapter I summarize the main points that came to light (anyone interested in the full picture has only to write to me for a full transcript):

- Panic, wanting to die at not knowing anything about what is being assessed.

- Making the wrong choice of first question (exams) – a good start is essential!

- Humiliation and feeling of inadequacy.

- Exam paper format is different from that expected. The main topics I studied do not appear at all in the paper. The fire alarm goes off!

- Arriving late, ill prepared, not being able to answer any questions.

- Freezing, mind going blank, realizing afterwards (and too late) what I ought to have said or written.

- Humiliation, 'moral' judgement on me (not just my work).

- Fear, panic, not being asked what I had studied. The awful gut feeling that you wake up with on the morning of the exam – still remembered several years later.

- Sick, calamity, foolishness, career up the spout, panic.

- Being so tense that I might pass out, and suffer the embarrassment of being carried out of the exam room.

- Finding that I was so strung up, that despite the fact I knew how to answer the question, I just could not get my hand steady enough to write the answer.

- Not prepared, exposed, found to be ignorant.

- Totally unexpected questions in a viva situation – misunderstanding the assessment criteria.

- (About continuous assessment) Fear that I haven't handed in a piece of (assessed) coursework (still a recurring dream) that I didn't know about or forgot about.

- (Continuous assessment): Why me? – my essay was as good/bad as anyone else's. It's not fair. Humiliation – I was pulled out in front of my class and asked to read the essay.

- (Driving test): Being assessed by a person who was described to me as 'a bugger'. Being assessed by a person who had failed me twice before.

It is salutary to compare the catalogue of horrors above to the 'wanting, doing, feedback and digesting' model of how people learn best. Most of these nightmares show the 'want' badly damaged or threatened, the 'learning by doing' experience at its most hostile and uncomfortable, the 'feedback' element either absent or negative, and the conditions anything but suitable for 'digestion'.

EXAMS VERSUS CONTINUOUS ASSESSMENT: COMPARISON OF FEELINGS

I asked delegates to jot down key words about their respective feelings about exams and continuous assessment. Below, I have summarized the data they wrote on their post-its. Several words (such as 'anxiety') occurred many times. It should also be noted that many of the positive and negative words occur under each of the headings 'exams' and 'continuous assessment'. When asked, 'How many of you actually enjoyed exams?' a handful of conference delegates admitted that they had done so. However, at an educational conference, it may be speculated that most of the members of the audience had been successful in exams already, whether they enjoyed them or not.

Emotions and feelings about exams

Positive feelings made up about a quarter of all the reported emotions. They included:

> adrenaline surge; culmination; peaking; excited; challenge; half-confident; relaxed – confident in writing; sense of relief after exam; relief (when there's something I can do); confidence about doing well; focused; fun; thrill; game; quickly over; secure; nothing unexpected; triumph; fear, then release; glad it would be over soon.

Negative feelings outweighed them, comprising almost three-quarters of the reports. They included:

> nervous; pressure; fear; panic; strain; what if my mind goes blank?; frustration; tension; pressure; anxiety; at a crossroads; claustrophobic; short-termist; cramming; exhaustion; risk; unsure what I was being assessed for; panic; scary; end point; last chance; apprehensive; anxious to plan pace effectively; boredom of revision; under pressure; hate; tired; edgy; keyed-up; worried; disadvantaged; boredom; jumping hurdles; helpless; passive; frustration; anger; surface approach; cram; total depression.

Feelings about continuous assessment

There is evidence of a lot of 'stress' and 'pressure' in delegates' recollections of their feelings about continuous assessment, but also an equal amount of evidence of a feeling of greater control, greater fairness and even pleasure. Again, I think it is interesting to see examples of the range of feelings, and worth remembering that most post-it contributions contained a mixture of positive and negative feelings at once, reflecting the overall 50/50 split between positive and negative feelings.

Positive feelings included:

> not such a high level of pressure; in control; chance to excel with no time barrier; more individuality; more enjoyable; chance to develop my work; pleasure; work; anxious; relaxed; interested; aware of ongoing progress; impressed; wishing to do my best; the chance to do right things I previously did wrong; opportunity to improve; involved in my work; more scope for originality; learned a lot from it; research; discovery; partnership; linked closely with learning material; in control.

Negative feelings included:

> chore; stressful; pointless; ongoing load; time-consuming; procras-
> tination; nuisance – got in the way, because it didn't count; slow,
> defensive; fairly anxious; burdensome; never-ending; tense; unsure;
> here we go again; wary; need to keep achieving.

'GUT FEELINGS' ABOUT LEARNING PAY-OFF

On the same post-it on which delegates had recorded their emotions and
feelings about exams and continuous assessment, I asked them to record
their subjective feelings about how effective (or otherwise) on a scale of
0–100 three aspects of assessment had felt to them. Under each heading I
have shown how they rated their experience of assessment.

Learning pay-off from actually doing assessed coursework

Most delegates related the learning pay-off from assessed coursework
between 60 and 90 as productive in terms of learning. However, a few
delegates indicated that they had not experienced assessed coursework,
and had only been assessed by exams.

Mark on scale 1–100	0–19	20–39	40–59	60–79	80–100
% responses	3	5	11	40	41

Learning pay-off from preparing for exams

The learning pay-off from *preparing for* exams was rated highly by many
delegates, but not (on average) quite as highly as for doing assessed
coursework.

Mark on scale 1–100	0–19	20–39	40–59	60–79	80–100
% responses	8	16	27	25	24

Learning pay-off from doing exams

Not surprisingly, the learning pay-off from actually doing exams tended
to be low – often zero.

Mark on scale 1–100	0–19	20–39	40–59	60–79	80–100
% responses	42	34	12	6	6

However, it must be remembered that this needs to be coupled with the learning pay-off associated with the preparation for exams shown above. It is worth thinking about ways that may increase the actual amount of learning involved in doing exams as well as preparing for them.

TEN WORRIES ABOUT EXAMS

In bringing together thoughts about the comparative merits and limitations of the two main varieties of assessment, I addressed ten concerns I have about each (these concerns are covered in greater detail elsewhere [Race, 1994b] and a much fuller account of many of these concerns is provided in Brown and Knight, 1994):

1   Exams don't do much to warm up the 'want to learn'.

2   Exams are not ideal occasions for 'learning by doing'.

3   The amount of feedback that learners receive about their exam performance is minimal.

4   Exams don't help learners make sense of what they've learned.

5   We mark exam scripts in a rush.

6   When we mark exams, we're often tired and bored.

7   We're not particularly good at marking objectively.

8   Exams tend to favour candidates who happen to be good at doing exams.

9   Exams encourage surface learning – and rapid 'clearing' ready for the next one.

10   Exams only measure some things – and often fail to measure more important qualities.

TEN WORRIES ABOUT CONTINUOUS ASSESSMENT

Despite the advantages of continuous assessment that delegates listed on their post-it contributions, many people's experience of continuous assessment remains far from positive. My principal concerns are:

1 Learners can feel under so much pressure that their 'want to learn' is damaged.

2 Though 'learning by doing' may be involved, the range of 'doing' may be quite narrow (for example, writing essays).

3 The value of feedback is often eclipsed by learners' reactions to scores or grades.

4 Learners rarely have time or opportunity to 'make sense' of the experience or the feedback.

5 The opportunity for tutors to give learners good feedback is reduced by large class sizes.

6 In large classes, the chances of cheating not being noticed are higher.

7 Learners don't usually know much about the criteria being used to assess their work.

8 When there are exams and continuous assessment, learners may spend too much time on the latter – and even fail their exams.

9 Student life becomes driven by assessment, instead of by learning.

10 Too little use is made of the enormous potential for learners to learn by assessing.

TEN PRINCIPLES OF ASSESSMENT

These principles have emerged from the work of an Assessment Issues Group organized by the Open Learning Foundation. This is in fact the fourth version of the issues and has been modified and refined on the basis of feedback gathered from a wide range of universities and practitioners in various subject disciplines.

1 The purposes of assessment need to be clear.

2 Assessment needs to be an integral part of course design, not something to be bolted on afterwards.

3 Assessment methodology needs to be valid.

4 Assessment processes and instruments need to be reliable.

5 Assessment methodology needs to be feasible.

6 Assessment needs to be transparent to students, staff and employers.

7   Assessment needs to be a means of delivering feedback.

8   The overall assessment strategy needs to employ a wide range of techniques and processes.

9   The amount of assessment should be appropriate.

10   Assessment should be free of bias.

It can be argued that each of these principles is somewhat vague, and that however laudable the intentions are, there is not sufficient detail in them. However, the Assessment Issues Group is developing a 'Personal Assessment Audit Checklist', based on these principles, in which a series of questions is intended to help teaching staff (and others) reach conclusions about the extent to which assessment systems and instruments are compatible with each principle.

RECOMMENDATIONS FOR IMPROVING ASSESSMENT

The purpose of the final interactive episode in my presentation was to harness the wide range of expertise and experience in the audience, and help to turn it into practical recommendations to improve assessment. I suggested that recommendations should be linked where possible to the four principal stages in learning that I had outlined earlier in the session. I also suggested that the recommendations should be targeted at different groups:

- policy makers
- quality auditors
- managers
- funding bodies
- teaching staff.

Not surprisingly, the number of recommendations to teaching staff far exceeded those to the other target groups – it is probably teaching staff who are in a position to do more about improving assessment than anyone else. To avoid over-burdening this chapter with lists and keeping in mind the readership of this book, I have not given details of the suggestions for auditors and funding bodies separately, although they are incorporated in my first, general list.

Many of the recommendations overlap, and it is very hard to keep them tightly to the respective headings and target groups. However, I have attempted to sum up the large quantity of recommendations produced by delegates in as logical a sequence as possible. There were general recommendations pertaining to all five groups. These are listed first.

Recommendations to all five groups, under all four headings

- Ask each audience what are their assessment policies, strategies, principles, guidelines, code of practice.

- Ask each audience to justify each element of their policy, strategy, principles, guidelines, code of practice.

- Ask each audience how they are attaining and living up to each of the elements above.

- (In other words, we need criterion-referenced self- and peer-assessment for the assessors).

- Recognize and acknowledge the reality of subjectivity in assessment, and the pretence of objectivity.

- Recognize and acknowledge the value (and inevitability) of self-assessment. (In other words, self-assessment happens all the time anyway, so bring it to the fore and use it).

- Advocate a role for educationalists as supporters and facilitators of self-assessment (not just teachers).

- Move away from 'top-down' models of assessment, and involve students and teachers in devising assessment systems and criteria.

- Invite institutions and departments to specify how their assessments and exams address 'the want to learn', learning by doing, learning from feedback, and making sense of what has been learned.

- Assessment must be made to be part of the learning experience; if not, it is time wasted.

- Promote the idea of self-assessment, and value this skill (and reward it).

- Remember that much learning takes place that is never taught, and never assessed.

- Require clear assessment criteria, written and negotiated with students.

- Communicate clearly – don't assume that they know what you want.

- Cultivate a climate of openness and trust.

Recommendations to policy makers

Changing assessment to amplify 'the want to learn'

- Students should have an opportunity to develop and be assessed on their interests which are not part of the curriculum but which may be relevant to their future careers.

- Give students the option to choose the forms of assessment most appropriate for them.

- Forget about norm-referencing.

- Require that every piece of assessed work is justified in some way towards 'wanting to learn', 'learning by doing' 'learning from feedback' or 'making sense of what is learned' – otherwise junk the assessments and the resultant data!

- Scrap degree classification systems, and introduce pass/fail systems and learner-directed learning.

- Keep student learning as the objective of assessment. Standardizing is only a second-order objective.

Changing assessment to help people to 'learn by doing'

- Think again: exactly what is a degree?

- Make exams optional for staff and students.

Changing assessment to help people to benefit from feedback

- Stop pressing performance indicators which rely on degree scores, final grades, and so on.

- Make competence in assessment a requirement for entry into higher education teaching.

- Make attendance at in-service professional development workshops on assessment a requirement for pay increments.

Changing assessment to help people to 'digest' what they learn

- Stop thinking about accelerated degree programmes (the 'digesting' is certain to be the part of learning which is restricted).

- Encourage the use of portfolios and records of achievement.

Recommendations to managers

Changing assessment to amplify 'the want to learn'

- Give some choices (of assessment forms) – involve students.

- Look for a range of assessments. Look for feedback systems, and student evaluation of the quality of the feedback they receive.

- Coordinate assessment in a modular framework.

Changing assessment to help people to 'learn by doing'

- To prepare their own appraisal portfolios in a manner consistent with their expectations of how students should prepare portfolios.

- Encourage assessment which is practical and 'real'.

- Managers who nominate staff to attend courses that have assessed course work, should play an active part in the assessment process. They should reinforce the processes of staff development and sharing learning and teaching with their staff.

Changing assessment to help people to benefit from feedback

- Ensure that student personal tutors and academic counsellors have access to all the assessment grades (using a common database) for each student and each tutor, so that academic counselling can be informed. This necessitates grades to be collected throughout the semester.

- Involve self- and peer-feedback. Include on-the-spot feedback from practical sessions.

- Try to instil student confidence at the earliest opportunity – give early feedback on relatively straightforward tasks.

- Require that assessment criteria are available to students before they undertake assessment.

- Enable (oblige?) teaching staff to become skilled at writing clear learning outcomes for their modules/programmes, through induction or INSET programmes on assessing in higher education.

Changing assessment to help people to 'digest' what they learn

- Use assessments which enable students to problem-solve and apply their skills.

- If you want to use self- and peer-assessment with students, take the opportunity to give them the same training as assessors – it's easy to forget that the ability to act as an assessor isn't something that we can take for granted in others. Perhaps it needs to be taught, not caught.

● Give staff enough time to ensure that they can give appropriate amounts of time to giving feedback and going through it with students.

Recommendations to teaching staff

Changing assessment to amplify 'the want to learn'

● Train students in assessment techniques so that they may become better managers of their own learning, and are aware of how they themselves can assess their learning.

● Make continuous assessment very 'real life'.

● Be open to new approaches; think about students' learning rather than your own performance or convenience.

● Try to develop skills to help students *share* assessment tasks and criteria, rather than approaching assessment as a timed, competitive activity.

● Make sure that your students have some ownership of the process – for example, ensure that they have a say in the tasks they do, how they are assessed, who assesses.

● Get rid of final exams, retain in-course time-limited assignments.

● Include learners' feelings in assessment.

● Make a drastic reduction in the amount of coursework set.

● Build into course documentation precise details of how assessment works.

● Give more detailed feedback on work, not just scores.

● Make more effort to enable and support peer support groups among learners (also helping them to reflect and digest their learning).

● Remember that learning is the objective of education, not assessment.

Changing assessment to help people to 'learn by doing'

● Use learning contracts.

● Use 'what I learnt from doing that' tasks to help learners reflect on and assess group tasks.

- Increase the proportion of marks given to coursework.

- Use short formative assessments, initially with rapid feedback.

- Involve students in designing assessment tasks.

- Don't bolt assessment on – tie it in to course design.

- Concentrate on quality rather than quantity, both in assessing and in learning.

- Identify the skills and processes in each subject which students are intended to become able to *do*, and build round these assessment strategies which are appropriate and relevant.

- Develop assessment formats other than 'traditional essays' such as posters, solving real problems, making videos.

- Put students in control of their learning by getting them to set questions and answer them.

Changing assessment to help people to benefit from feedback

- Reduce the time interval before feedback is given.

- Consult more with students – give them some input into policies and structures of assessment.

- Make feedback immediate (for example using computer feedback).

- Allow all assessed work to be returned to students.

- Give detailed feedback on all examinations to all students (if you must have exams).

- Help teachers themselves to get more feedback by encouraging peer observation of teaching.

- Ban 'model solutions' and get feedback to students in better ways.

- Use self- and peer-assessment.

- Give marked finals papers back to students. (I've tried to make this happen in my own university – but so far without success [except for my own exams!])

- Build in self-assessment and reflection into assessment criteria.

- Talk to each other about what you are looking for in an assessment.

- Learn how to frame your feedback so that it is meaningful, usable, constructive and interesting to students.

- Give feedback on drafts of essays – get students to agree the agenda for work.

Changing assessment to help people to 'digest' what they learn

- Move away from the need to assess each component part of a course by developing a team strategy distributing the mode and character of forms of assessment among members of course teams (leading to students having a richer variety of experiences to help them 'digest' their learning).

- Use a mock exam and debrief thoroughly a month before finals.

- Trust students to give one another feedback and to learn from it – in a safe 'no fail' situation. Build in debriefing.

- Return exam scripts to learners and get them to use the feedback in some way – for example, seek clarification, write themselves a learning contract on the basis of the feedback they receive.

Funding bodies and quality auditors

In a nutshell, the recommendations to these two groups are that they should align their policies so as to recognize, reward and promote best assessment practice. There was sharp awareness that the agendas they set have considerable potential to improve the quality of learning in universities. There was also a feeling that they are not yet ready to use this power to improve student learning by means of encouraging better assessment methods.

CONCLUSIONS

After a set of recommendations so powerful and diverse as those listed above, it is clear that there is much to be done to move towards a state where assessment plays a full and positive part in the learning experience of our students in higher education. The fact that these recommendations have been collected from conference delegates who are at the sharp end of the development of good teaching and learning practices in higher education adds a great deal of authority and credibility to their words. I hope that their experience and wisdom, as embodied in this chapter, will be put to good use by all of the 'target groups' we addressed in our thinking.

Chapter 5

Using and Experiencing Assessment

Sally Brown, Phil Race and Chris Rust

INTRODUCTION

Many of us working in higher education regard assessment as being a crucial element of the learning process, and yet training is rarely given to lecturers new to the profession or wishing to develop their assessing abilities further, on how to assess well in order to help students to focus their activities and learn more effectively. All three of us run workshops and other forms of training in which the experience of undertaking assessment activities and actually being assessed forms a substantial part of the programme.

This chapter explores some of the learning that can be derived from these kinds of workshops, drawing on our own experience and that of participants in our interactive sessions. To develop these ideas, here we pose a number of key questions that assessors should ask themselves and explore some appropriate responses.

HOW GOOD ARE YOU AT ASSESSING?

This first question is a crucial one, because we assert that assessors need to bring to the task of assessing the same level of self-evaluation and reflective practice that we often require of learners. Because we happen to be employed in positions where part of the work is to award learners grades or marks for their work, it is easy to suppose that we are capable of doing this part of our work competently and almost automatically.

For much of the time the act of assessing is done quite privately; in other words, there is not much opportunity for lecturers to gain feedback about how well (or otherwise) they are assessing. It is often only when staff find themselves double-marking or working in parallel using agreed assessment schemes, that they discover the frightening truth that assessment tends to be subjective and unreliable. The following checklist of questions is intended to help you to conduct a self-appraisal. Use it to evaluate how effective your system is and change your strategies accordingly.

- Have you sufficient time to devote to assessing?

- Are you able to formulate clear assessment criteria for each piece of work you assess, making assessment as objective and fair as possible?

- Are you able to share assessment criteria with learners? For example, can you agree assessment criteria in advance when setting course-work?

- Can you share past assessment criteria with learners so that they can see how their work is assessed?

- Can you work with colleagues so that you have someone else's ratings of a cross-section of your students' work, and are alerted to any area where your assessment may not be ideal?

- Is it possible for you to involve learners in self-assessment of their own work by providing them with clear, understandable marking schemes and criteria? This helps learners think more deeply about their work than if they simply handed it to you to mark. Scanning how well learners have self-assessed an exercise and commenting on particular points takes much less time than marking it all yourself.

- Can you build peer-assessment into the coursework elements of your subject? Peer-assessment helps learners to understand what the 'rules of the assessment game' are, but (more importantly) allows them to derive a great deal of useful feedback from each other.

- Are you able to participate in assessing that is necessarily moderated and checked – for example A-level scripts? Having to stick closely to an agreed assessment scheme is one of the best ways to learn how to make your own assessment schemes rigorous and fair.

WHAT ARE WE ASSESSING?

A key question that needs to be asked before even starting is, what are we assessing? Do we know, and *do the learners* know? If we are assessing an essay, for example, are we assessing the content, the style, or the pre-sentation? And if some combination of these, with what weighting to each?

And are we assessing the product, or the process that produced it? The former may be fine if this is a summative exercise, at the end of a course, whose major purpose is to decide who should fail or pass, and with what degree classification. On the other hand, if the assessment is to serve a formative function, that is to assist learners to do better next time, we need to examine the process that led to the product. Seeing a first draft, and then a revised version of the essay, supported by a reading log, for example, can be a really powerful developmental process. There is also the question of whether skills, such as leadership, or the ability to work in a group, are to be assessed.

WHY ARE WE ASSESSING?

Among the many reasons for undertaking the task of assessment that we have identified in our workshops, these are some of the most important:

- to provide feedback to learners so they can learn from mistakes and build on achievements

- to classify or grade student achievement

- to enable learners to correct errors and remedy deficiencies

- to motivate learners and to focus their sense of achievement

- to consolidate student learning

- to help learners to apply abstract principles to practical contexts

- to estimate students' potential to progress to other levels or courses

- to guide selection or option choice

- to give us feedback on how effective we are being at promoting learning

- to provide statistics for internal and external agencies.

Set against these positive reasons for assessment, we should also consider whether our reasons for our choices about what and how we assess also include tradition ('we've always done it this way'), inertia ('why should we change how we are doing it?') and a desire to control ('learners will just have to buckle down and do what they are told!').

In order to assess well, we need to clarify for ourselves and for our learners what the specific purposes of an assessment activity are and to design it accordingly.

HOW CAN WE MAKE ASSESSMENT FAIR? WHERE DO OBJECTIVITY AND SUBJECTIVITY FIT IN?

The enemy is the tendency to put down the number (or grade) we first thought of. There will always remain a degree of subjectivity in assessing, but the effect is greatly reduced by the processes of formulating clear criteria, and working out a detailed marking scheme showing exactly how many marks go to each element of students' work. An analogy could be that using a detailed assessment scheme is similar to measuring the temperature with a long, fine thermometer with clear gradations showing every tenth of a degree. Probably the fastest way to check the objectivity of our assessment is to get two or three colleagues to double-mark samples, and then to discuss differences. We would argue that an even better way is to make assessment public by sharing marking schemes and assessment criteria with learners, and allowing them to discuss the interpretation of the criteria as reflected in the marks that are awarded to them.

HOW SHOULD WE ASSESS ARTEFACTS? (AND SCIENTEFACTS AND ENGINEEREFACTS!)

In many subject areas it is necessary to assess objects and other items that have been produced by the learners, for example sculptures, engineering products, designs, plans, fashion garments, photographs, models and other artefacts. In these cases, it is even more important that the brief to which the student is working is crystal-clear both to the student and the assessor. Where there is no shared agreement on this, often judgements made can be based largely on subjectivity and good old 'gut reaction', often cloaked by the term 'experience'.

One very good way of ensuring that learners are working on the right lines is to give them, if possible, lots of examples of previously submitted artefacts for them to appraise. By looking at examples of both highly rated and low-marked items and by discussing the qualities that make them so with the tutor and with peers, learners are more likely to build up a sense of what is to be achieved and what constitutes successful practice.

HOW CAN WE GET THE ASSESSMENT RIGHT?

Assessment criteria need to be explicit, and understood by everyone, staff and learners. Simply issuing them along with the task is better than nothing, but it doesn't ensure that they are understood. What exactly is meant by 'analysis', for example? Marking exercises, using the criteria, and seeing examples of marked work, with accompanying comments, are two ways in which the learners' understanding of the criteria can be developed.

This still leaves the question of ownership; if the criteria are those of the tutor, the learners may never feel quite as comfortable as they would have if they had participated in drawing them up. Involving the learners in deciding which criteria should be used to assess a particular task is an excellent exercise in developing their understanding of the whole assessment process, and should produce better work as a result.

One further issue connected to criteria is that of the level of work they demand. Some criteria can be satisfied by work of a low level. If the task and the criteria are undemanding, they may be satisfied perfectly (so should it receive an 'A'?) when it is really only C-grade work. One possible solution to this is to use range statements which give some indication of the level of required achievement in specific contexts.

HOW CAN WE WEIGHT CRITERIA TO FOCUS STUDENT ACTIVITY APPROPRIATELY?

This works best when learners themselves have been involved in formulating a set of assessment criteria for a task they are about to start (for example, preparing to give a presentation, or to write a particular report, or to put together essays on a given theme). However, even if it is necessary to supply learners with the assessment criteria as a *fait accompli*, it is still useful to get learners to negotiate how best to weight them. An effective way of doing this is as follows. Suppose seven assessment criteria have been formulated:

- Write the criteria up on a flipchart or overhead slide, so all of the class can see all of the criteria simultaneously.

- Go through each of the criteria, saying, 'What this *really* means is...' and adding one or two explanatory key words beneath each criterion, so that the whole group has a shared understanding of the meaning of the words used in the criteria.

- With groups of 40 or less: allocate a total score for the seven criteria (eg, 40 marks). Ask each member of the group individually and privately to split the 40 marks between the seven criteria. Remind them that they can award zero to any criterion they don't feel is important at all, and can give the lion's share of the 40 to a particularly important criterion if they wish. With groups of more than about 40 learners, it works well if you divide the class into groups so that *each group* can undertake the above process.

- Using an overhead transparency or flipchart, collect all the scores, in other words, ask everyone (or every group) for the score they awarded to each criterion, and collate them by working down the list.

- There will usually be a clear trend, seen through the numbers, showing which of the criteria are the most important ones. It is often well worth exploring with the learners why particular criteria scored high marks from some of them, and low marks from others – such discussions usually throw further light on the significance of the criteria and how best to interpret them.

- It is often possible to work out the average score for each criterion, which then becomes the weighting in the assessment scheme.

The process outlined above is particularly useful when learners will be engaged in applying the criteria to each other's work. Their shared understanding of the exact meaning of the criteria (and their ownership of the scoring scheme) combine to enhance the quality of their experience of peer-assessing.

WHO IS BEST PLACED TO ASSESS?

Having decided what is to be assessed, an important linked question is, 'Who can undertake that assessment most effectively?'

Traditionally, assessment has been carried out by tutors and if what is being assessed is a product such as an essay, they may be the best people to do this. However, since we assert that involving learners in the process may actually help to develop their own judgemental skills, and thereby improve future performance, self- and peer-assessment can fulfil an important, formative function.

Moreover, if certain skills or aspects of the process are being assessed, then the tutor may not be in any position to make a judgement. For example, learners themselves may be the only ones who can assess what has actually been learned or gained from carrying out a particular task. This might be accessed through a piece of reflective writing, for example. If, however, individual students' contributions to a group project are to be assessed, they may not be as well placed to make a sound judgement as the peers with whom they have been working.

HOW CAN WE USE ASSESSMENT TO EMPOWER LEARNERS?

Assessment systems where the responsibility for assessment lies squarely in the hands of tutors, with the learners as passive recipients of judgements handed down to them by the tutor, can make learners feel powerless. When assessment is done in secret, with tutors keeping to themselves the grounds upon which they make assessment decisions, learners can find themselves in a client role and this may breed distrust and a feeling of 'us and them'.

If we involve learners in their own assessment, or at least provide plenty of opportunities for learners to interrogate us and the criteria, this allows us to share power with them and they then tend to become more confident about their learning as a whole. In workshops, really effective cooperative learning activities can be enhanced by examining the seemingly arbitrary nature of tutor assessment. Where participants are asked to undertake a task and the products are assessed by the tutor, it is often the case that they query the authority of the tutor, especially if they are involved in self- and peer-assessment.

HOW CAN ASSESSMENT IMPROVE LEARNING?

The key to the use of assessment as an engine for learning is to allow the formative function to be pre-eminent. This is achieved by ensuring that each assignment contains plenty of opportunities for learners to receive detailed, positive and timely feedback, with lots of advice on how to improve. This not only informs student activity, but also enables them to develop continuously and to achieve ever-better results. Where pressures on tutor time make high levels of tutor feedback impractical, we would again argue for the use of self- and peer-assessment. Because they are regularly being asked to make evaluative comments about their own and each other's work, learners participating in these methods learn a lot about the processes of assessment and of learning, and this gives them insights into ways of improving their work.

HOW CAN WE ENSURE RELIABILITY AND VALIDITY?

These words are used widely in discussions on the quality of assessment. However, they often mean rather different things to different people. It is useful to qualify each of these terms with these checklist questions:

Reliability

- Would different assessors award the same marks or grades to each student?
- Is the assessment scheme one which is fair to all learners?

Validity

- Does the assessment scheme reflect the published aims, learning outcomes, objectives or competence outcomes of the course?

- Is the assessment measuring the 'right things'? In other words, is the assessment addressing the skills and competences which learners are intended to develop, rather than being over-influenced by (for example) the flair with which learners write essays?

- Is the assessment scheme practically feasible?

HOW CAN WE GET THE STATISTICS RIGHT?

In turning assessment into marks, it is vitally important that tutors take account of the following issues and to remember that assessment, at best, is a very inexact science:

- If assessment criteria are each allocated specific scores, the overall mark will almost certainly go up (grade inflation).

- If learners have been significantly involved in setting the assessment tasks and criteria, performance may be generally better and marks higher overall as a result.

- If groups are assessed, there may be a regression to the mean, because weaker learners are likely to be brought up by the abilities of others in the group, and more able learners may have their marks brought down by less able colleagues.

- With an increase in modular courses and continuous assessment schemes, problems can occur in relation to overall course marks, when like is not being added to like. Marks originating from different elements or aspects of an assignment are frequently just added together, and averaged with, other marks derived from entirely different contexts, and this can skew the final total in a disproportionate way.

Often the most appropriate outcome of an assessment activity is not a simple mark or grade, but a descriptive profile of achievement, which gives a more complete breakdown of what a student knows or can do, perhaps in the form of a record of achievement which can be used for admission, in charting personal development within a programme of study and in seeking employment on graduation (Knight, 1995).

WHAT ABOUT ASSESSING GROUPS?

There are good reasons for setting group tasks and assessing groups:

● it can help to develop a range of important skills

● more can be achieved by a group than by an individual

● there is often less marking and therefore less demand on resources.

Where assessment is used formatively, learners may be involved in assessing the products of other peer groups (inter-peer group assessment) or in assessing the processes by which their own group members have interacted (intra-peer group assessment).

When it comes to marking and summative assessment, whether self-, peer- or tutor-assessment is used, there is always the problem of how to make group assessment fair, given the opportunity for some learners to ride on the backs of others. This may actually be more an imagined problem than a real one; it is most important to have a clearly stated mechanism which specifically deals with this, even if in reality it can only be partially successful. Some possible mechanisms that do this are described in detail in Brown *et al.* (1994, Ch. 6).

There is still considerable argument about whether students' ability successfully to evaluate themselves and their peers is affected by factors such as race, age and gender. Such evidence as exists is contradictory: Gibbs (1991) argues that female trainee teachers on a postgraduate certificate at Oxford Brookes University tended to under-rate themselves in relation to the males, whereas Race (1994b) says that he noticed no such bias. The important learning point seems to be that self- and peer-assessment need rehearsal and negotiation before implementation in a mark-bearing context. There must also be substantial reliance (as in all methods of assessment) on the use of appropriate and published criteria, supported by appropriate evidence.

WHY SHOULD WE BUILD IN VARIETY INTO OUR ASSESSMENT PRACTICES?

Perhaps the most powerful criticism that can be levelled at traditional approaches to assessment is that students' grades or degree classifications depend too much on a limited set of abilities, including:

● their skill at delivering written exam answers against the clock

● their ability to 'keep their cool' under time pressure and in an unfriendly environment

- their skill at writing stylishly, over and above the actual content.

If assessment is to be a useful part of the learning experience of learners, it is useful to employ a fairly diverse variety of assessment types and formats. Not only do we need a range of assessment methods if we are to assess a range of competences, but also we should remember that all forms of assessment discriminate in some way against some groups of learners. Using a good range of assessment methods also brings variety to students' learning experiences.

A wide variety of types of assessment exists and is described in more detail by Brown and Knight (1994). Methods include:

- activities putting into perspective a topic or issue

- case studies and simulations

- critical reviews of articles, viewpoints or opinions

- critiques

- dissertations and theses

- essay plans (almost as much thinking can go into making these as into writing full essays)

- essays, formal and non-traditional

- fieldwork, casework and other forms of applied research

- laboratory reports and notebooks

- literature searches (for example the preparation of annotated bibliographies)

- in-tray exercises

- oral presentations

- poster exhibitions

- practical skills and competences

- projects (individual, or group)

- reviews for specific audiences

- seen written exams (where learners have the questions in advance)

- strategic plans (testing higher-order skills than can usually be tested in exams)

- unseen written exams (too many of these still exist!)

CONCLUSIONS

Participants in our workshops often describe how being assessed on the outcomes of a task, however small-scale, helps them to remember all the feelings and negative responses they associated with assessment in their own learning histories. Our aim, both in workshop sessions and in this chapter, is to promote a more strategic approach to assessment in which tutors clarify in advance the purposes and required outcomes of any assignment, then design assignments accordingly so that they really achieve what they set out to do. Assessment then can promote active learning, rather than being a rather sterile, end-point activity, useful only to pigeonhole learners and to maintain the status quo.

Chapter 6

Making Assessment a Positive Experience

Bob Farmer and Diana Eastcott

How can we make assessment a positive experience for students? The purpose of this chapter is to investigate ways in which the principles of good assessment identified by Phil Race in Chapter 4 have been applied in practice. Most of the applications are based on suggestions from participants at the final session of the Assessment for Learning in Higher Education Conference. Participants were asked to identify those ideas and strategies for positive assessment which they had come across at the conference and would want to take back to their own institutions to share with their students and colleagues.

We have grouped the applications of good assessment practice broadly according to Race's practical model, which identifies the key processes for successful learning as being wanting, doing, digesting and feedback.

- Wanting to learn is at the heart of the process with ways of encouraging positive feelings and the urge to want to learn. This is the centre of Race's model of learning.

- Learning by doing is linked with feedback: for the purposes of this chapter we have linked these two parts of the model of learning.

- Digesting – ways of giving students opportunities for making sense of what they are learning through a process of digestion and reflection.

WANTING TO LEARN

It is often claimed that assessment drives learning and that without some form of testing most students would not bother to do very much work. While this may be true, in practice students come on our courses with very different levels of motivation and a variety of reasons for wanting to study. At one extreme, with some externally assessed professional courses, the wanting is extrinsically derived. Students are looking for vocational qualifications. There is no time for learning-by-doing and strategies for encouraging deep approaches and reflection can be counter-productive in terms of the all-important quest for passing externally marked examinations and gaining a qualification. As tutors we may have very little control over situations such as this. Often the best we can do is to help our students to go along with the system. However, when, as in the majority of cases, we are in a position to influence students' desires to want to learn, the opportunities are not always taken. Traditional methods prevail and assessment is often seen by staff and students alike as a necessary bolt-on activity for establishing levels of achievement at the end of a course.

One issue frequently touched upon was the need to examine closely the learning context in which students find themselves in the first few weeks of a course. Expectations of assessment requirements in these early stages can have a crucial influence on the nature and levels of motivation, and induction courses provide excellent opportunities for clarifying departmental and institutional teaching, learning and assessment strategies. Some of the practical suggestions made at the conference are discussed here.

Explicit discussion with students about the nature of learning in relation to the subjects being studied

One strategy for doing this involved briefing the students on the work of Marton and Saljo (1976; 1984) about the nature of surface and deep approaches to learning and, where appropriate, using a shortened version of the *Approaches to Studying Questionnaire* developed at Edinburgh as a means of encouraging students to reflect upon their current approaches. (A copy of the questionnaire and an account of its use in a number of different learning contexts is given in *Improving the Quality of Student Learning*, Gibbs, 1992). Care is needed in the use of this instrument, since students could wrongly construe the results as a test of their learning ability. However, the questionnaire was found to have considerable potential when used as a way of explaining the learning strategies that tutors were hoping to encourage and also as an introduction to what some students might otherwise have seen as unconventional assessment procedures.

Making explicit the criteria on which students' assignments or performance will be judged

This is a recurring theme (see Chapter 1, for example). Having a clear understanding, as a learner, of where one is going and what one is expected to be able to do affects students' desire to learn. One workshop examined ways of relating current to future learning so as to help learners to have a sense of the meaning of what they are doing and to appreciate its significance.

Students' knowledge of learning and assessment criteria is particularly important in courses which employ criterion-referenced assessments designed to show specifically what the person can do rather than comparing one person with another. Without careful briefing, students can become disorientated and confused by assessments which demand displays of mastery and excellence together with expectations of high pass rates. One workshop explored the idea of running assessment simulations as part of student induction as a means of overcoming this type of problem.

A number of conference papers looked at positive ways of involving students in establishing their own assessment and learning criteria. Inherent in these strategies was a belief that it is advantageous for learners to feel some ownership of their learning, which might be encouraged through group work and peer-assessment.

LEARNING-BY-DOING LINKED WITH FEEDBACK

There was a lot of evidence from Phil Race's opening exercise at the conference (see Chapter 4) that delegates saw examinations as damaging to the 'learning-by-doing' experience, since the 'doing' in preparation for exams may often consist of acquiring information in ways that are frequently not conducive to digesting and understanding. Examinations were also seen as a poor way of providing feedback. The traditional strategy for overcoming these problems has been to introduce programmes of continuous assessment. However, despite the more obvious advantages of encouraging higher levels of student involvement, many delegates felt that today's large class sizes linked in some subject areas with opportunities for cheating, were cause for very genuine concern about the viability of continuous assessment.

A number of strategies for encouraging genuinely productive learning-by-doing linked with feedback emerged from the conference workshops; these included the following.

Developing patterns of assessment that encourage productive learner activity and feedback

In some subjects areas, such as mathematics for engineering or business studies, students' lack of motivation presented tutors with considerable difficulties and it was only by experimenting with different patterns of assessment that working solutions were found. Often these difficulties were associated with modular courses and large student numbers and where assessment through end-of-course closed-book exams pre-dominates. Inevitably, this assessment pattern failed to inspire very much wanting or doing on the part of the students. (The 'doing' in this instance consisting of regular practice in closed-ended problem solving.) High failure and referral rates are a common feature on these courses and a range of assessment patterns designed to address these issues was explored at the conference. These included:

- So-called 'fast feedback' tests which are peer marked in class and which encourage students to practise in their own time.

- Final assessment activities which take questions exclusively from pre-vious feedback tests.

- Assignments which focus on information gathering and analysis and which lead students to investigate more open-ended problems.

- Design questions, often involving computer packages, for the students to do in their own time, where they can talk to each other and discuss the principles involved. To avoid problems of plagiarism, learners are assessed not on the designs as much as on their ability to apply the designs in controlled conditions so as to solve problems. An accounts package for a small hotel might be designed by accountancy students and they would be assessed on their ability to apply it successfully to handle data given to them under examination conditions.

- Open-book assignment tests which assess students' understanding of the work set in an assignment (introduced in order to overcome problems with plagiarism).

A common theme in all of these discussions was the need to phase the delivery of the various elements of an assessment package so that testing could be successfully integrated into the learning process. Discussion also centred on the many practical issues to do with handling groups of mixed ability students, excessive marking and plagiarism.

Learner activity and feedback in groups

In contrast to the largely closed-ended learning described above, reports of students learning in groups were more usually associated with open-ended tasks and course units concerned with personal and interpersonal skills development. The provision of appropriate assessment procedures within the latter is crucial, but it is also difficult. We found that the message coming from a number of workshops and seminars was that unless carefully designed, any form of assessment in such areas can be very threatening to the individual and affect his or her desire to learn. It can also make it difficult to give supportive feedback. Students are nevertheless unlikely to give importance to these assignments if they do not properly count in the sense of having marks allocated to them in the overall degree classification process.

Where marks do count, ways should be considered for operating controlled peer assessment in which group members are given the responsibility for allocating a (small) percentage of the marks available to each individual. Opportunities should be taken to encourage self-assessment of personal/social skills prior to as well as after learning in groups. Students should be carefully inducted into programmes involving self- and peer-assessment.

A number of conference seminars examined assessment procedures within courses where lecture-based programmes had been supplanted by experiential units. Practical issues included the need to find ways of linking the process of learning on a module to its objectives. For example, students' levels of wanting to learn on an MA programme were greatly enhanced by finding ways of linking conceptual issues with the practical tasks of management that the participants were undertaking day to day. Group assessment tasks in this programme worked well because they supported the learning objectives of the course by rewarding students' ability to link theory with practice.

Using portfolios to encourage learner activity and feedback

Portfolios have long been a key assessment tool in the field of art and design. However, conference papers showed that they are increasingly used to support learning-by-doing in a variety of disciplines, including engineering, social work and business studies.

Portfolios should by their very nature encourage learning-by-doing and reflection. Conference seminars identified a number of positive features:

- they can provide evidence of what students have achieved in the workplace

- they are capable of encouraging 'want to learn' behaviour, particularly when students are encouraged to employ a variety of means of self-expression

- they can give students greater control over their own assessment

- they provide the tutor with an opportunity to monitor ongoing performance and progress, together with opportunities to give feedback

- they should encourage reflection and self-assessment.

Negative features were also identified. Some tutors reported that, if assignments are not carefully designed, students can be just as instrumental in their approach to the preparation of portfolios as they are to any other learning task.

DIGESTING

Race's definition of digesting as part of the learning process has many of the characteristics and attributes of reflective observation and abstract conceptualization described by Kolb (1984) in his famous learning cycle. Learners not only need to be given opportunities to make sense of what they are learning but they also require time to think about their own learning processes. Race also points out that we should be encouraging our students to make strategic decisions about what is important for them to retain and what is unimportant enough to be discarded. In other words, we need assessment strategies designed to help students make sense of what they are learning.

The conference provided a number of examples of courses designed to give students opportunities to reflect upon both the meaning of what they were learning and upon the process of learning itself.

In one course unit, students were persuaded to take the process of their own learning seriously by being required to evaluate the product of their reflection. This was achieved by requiring them to keep learning logs of what went well for them and what they needed to do in order to improve the way they tackled a particular assignment. They were then asked to submit a short essay, based on their learning log, to be handed in with the assignment as part of the assessment package.

A second case involved students being asked to develop their own criteria for the assessment of portfolio evidence, which was to be submitted towards a postgraduate qualification.

A third example employed tutor-designed marking sheets which outlined the criteria for assessment which students were required to use in order to grade themselves before returning their work for marking.

Assessment strategies designed to encourage students to help each other to learn

This looks at the benefits that come from having to explain things to another person and it is based on the notion that a most effective way of really getting to understand something is to teach it.

Two applications that emerged from the conference are:

● Small groups of three or four students had to plan and organize a learning session for the whole group. The students thus became teachers and not just presenters. They were then assessed on their contributions to all the seminar sessions by means of tutor observation, together with students' judgement of their individual and group statements.

● Using a peer feedback marking scheme to support and assess individual and group oral presentations.

SUMMARY

We have by no means exhausted the methods of assessment discussed at the conference. What we have tried to do, though, is to use Race's very practical ideas as a way of analysing good assessment practice. The four categories in the model are not imposed in a cyclic order: they overlap and interact with each other. They nevertheless help to provide us with a deceptively simple checklist of things to look out for when we design courses. They also remind us that assessment is at the core of course design, not least because 'how am I going to be tested?' is often at the very heart of students' approaches to and feelings about learning.

Chapter 7

Staff and Educational Development for Assessment Reform: A Case Study

Ivan Moore

Grant me the serenity to accept things I cannot change, courage to change things I can, and wisdom to know the difference.

(Attributed to Reinhold Niebuhr (1892–1971))

INTRODUCTION

Staff and educational development are about change; academic staff and institutional management cry out for stability; and the students want justice. All of us want to provide the best service possible, and the government wants efficiency gains. To add to this, we now also live and work in an increasingly competitive world. Openness and accountability mean that we are ever more exposed to the judgement of those in the general community who wish to judge us. And they do.

If these kinds of pressures are not sufficient, then we can add to them the movement of higher education towards a national matrix system. Modularization of courses, combined with developing expertise in Credit Accumulation and Transfer (CATs), the Accreditation of Prior Learning (APL), the Accreditation of Prior Experiential Learning (APEL) and the raft of National Vocational Qualifications (NVQs) force us into a system whereby we must be able to assess our incoming students against a wide range of qualifications. Of course, industry, commerce and the professions always had the challenge of comparing graduate qualifications from different universities, and now we too must be able to compare student levels of attainment from different institutions.

How often have you heard comments like:

Of course, a 2.1 honours from this university is equivalent to a first (or a 2.2) from ... university.

Mind you, it is far more difficult to get a first in physics than in history.

You know, standards are slipping. We must do something about it.

But what justification is there for it? Few university departments have explicit criteria and standards of achievement against which the students can be assessed and the idea of university-wide statements about desirable, cross-curricular learning outcomes is largely that – an idea. Fewer still make these standards available for external scrutiny. So we cannot compare standards across universities, or faculties, or through time.

So, if teaching reform is about quality and development, then assessment reform must in part be about fairness and stability. Of course there are many other aspects to assessment than fairness, but this single issue makes it a crucial area of concern and for action by staff and educational developers, academics and institutions.

Staff and educational developers are concerned with many aspects of teaching and learning. We carry out research into learning theory, we study works on teaching and learning, we collect teaching innovations, we network with other professionals in this area of work and we strive to maintain credibility by continuing to practise our trade wherever possible. But this alone is not enough. Indeed, it is very little, for we recognize all of this as a means to an end. However good we may become at teaching, however much valuable research we may carry out and however much we learn about the teaching and learning process, we will fall far short of the mark if we do not disseminate all of this 'expertise' to the staff in our own institutions and if we cannot create a culture and provide mechanisms within which change, where required, is a desirable and feasible outcome.

Of course, the scope of the work of staff and educational developers is very wide, which is suggested by Figure 7.1 showing factors influencing the prioritization of training needs. Depending on the mission of the university and the terms of reference of the development unit, activities can take place in areas as diffuse as teaching and learning, management, interpersonal skills, recruitment, equality, safety, quality systems and so on and it becomes difficult to prioritize the various needs. Even when the training needs are well defined, established and prioritized, departments still do not have sufficient information to determine training priorities. It is also necessary to determine the scale of these needs and the desire, or even willingness of staff to become involved in certain areas of development. We must also determine the potential benefits of the training and estimate the costs of this provision, both initial and recurrent. Will the institution be able to maintain the development or the outcome? Does it have the resources?

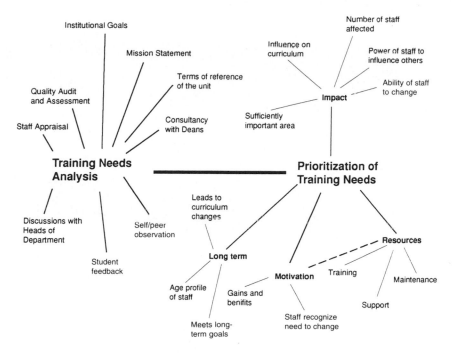

Figure 7.1   *Factors which influence the prioritization of identified training needs*

Finally, we must assess the likely outcomes of the programme. How effective will any development programme be in improving any area of activity? Is this area sufficiently important? What realistic gains can we expect to the performance of the individuals, departments and the institution as a whole?

Any development programme must be thoroughly researched and planned, but it should not be set in stone. It should be sufficiently well defined for everyone to understand it; it should be sufficiently firm to enable it to be carried through; and it should be sufficiently flexible to allow us to adapt to changing needs, externally imposed pressures and specific requests.

It is rare for a project to arise which meets all of the criteria for being accepted as a high priority programme and it is important to recognize one and to be able to make a quick and effective initial response. It is even more rare for such programmes to be initiated from outside the unit; for a request to be made from a department or faculty. When this happens it is essential to respond appropriately.

Figure 7.2 shows the relationship between the different levels of hierarchy in a university and the continuum of training needs. Requests from

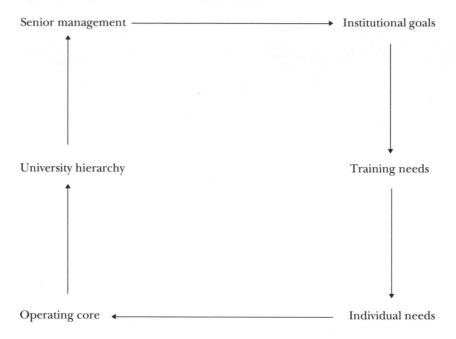

Figure 7.2   *Training needs vary according to the level of staff*

senior management tend to address needs that relate closely to institutional goals, whereas requests from the operating core tend to be aimed at meeting individual needs. Again, it is rare to encounter a request which has the potential to address the whole continuum for a significant number of staff.

CASE STUDY: DISCRIMINATION IN MARKING

In the spring of 1993, I received a memo from the secretary of the university's sub-committee on taught courses, chaired by the pro-vice chancellor for academic affairs. This memo expressed the committee's concern over the continuing problem of 'bunching of marks'. Simply expressed, the university felt that we did not produce enough first class honours degree students (and by implication that perhaps we did not produce enough thirds either!) I was then asked to consider whether Staff Development was in a position to provide some form of support for the committee in tackling this problem. I considered potential courses of action:

1. Ignore it!

2. Reply to indicate that we had a full schedule and wouldn't possibly have the resources to tackle the issue.

3. Send the committee some resource material on assessment (courtesy of SEDA).

4. Write a paper for the consideration of the committee, setting out the possible reasons for this bunching of marks and recommendations which they might wish to make to faculties.

5. Make some enquiries to try to find out more about the nature and extent of the problem.

6. Carry out research on assessment before responding.

7. Instigate a comprehensive and immediate programme of staff development on assessment.

I decided to follow option 5. I obtained from the committee secretary communications between the Academic Policy Committee and faculties. These communications went back over several years and indicated that the matter was more of an ongoing debate than an accepted problem. However, statistics produced by the university clearly indicated that the percentage of first class honours degrees awarded was much lower than the national average. Further, there was considerable variation both between and across faculties and from year to year. This allowed me to redefine the problem in two parts:

1. The university does not produce enough first class honours degree students.

2. There is inconsistency in the outcomes of our award structure, both temporally and across subjects.

I consulted a paper by the Dean of Education which suggested four factors which may contribute to the problem:

1. The intellectual calibre of the students.

2. The setting and marking of examination questions.

3. Variation in the range of marks awarded.

4. Regression to the mean.

Regression to the mean is a simple statistical phenomenon which occurs when averaging a set of marks. The averaging process smoothes out the highest and lowest marks and leads to a bunching around the mean mark. It can be overcome, at least in part, by a simple marks-stretching algorithm, if desired.

The intellectual calibre of the students is more or less fixed at entry, although A-level scores are by no means infallible predictors of university achievement. It might be more appropriate here to consider the effectiveness of our teaching and learning practices, that is to say, how well we build upon the achievements and the abilities that our students bring with them.

The second and third factors were identified as relating directly to assessment practice.

It was at this point that I responded to the committee by offering to devise a programme to tackle the problem and to present my ideas to them at their next meeting. This offer was accepted and I presented a paper on effective assessment.

The paper

The presentation was broken down into six sections:

- the context

- the problem redefined

- the role of Staff Development in tackling the problem

- the proposed programme

- the cost of the programme

- support material.

The context

This introduction covered the four factors listed by the Dean of Education (see above).

The problem redefined

The redefinition discussed the more fundamental issue of good assessment practice. It made the link between good assessment and effective teaching and learning; the issues and modes of assessment; and the philosophy of enabling the student to demonstrate ability.

The following section is taken directly from the presentation paper:

The discussion so far focuses on only one aspect of assessment and aims at increasing the spread of marks which will create more first class awards (and perhaps more third class).

A more fundamental approach should consider at least all aspects of assessment. Good assessment practice should ensure both validity and repeatability of the assessment. It is important to ensure that the assessment is linked with the teaching and learning objectives and desired student outcomes. Students should be aware of what is being assessed, why it is being assessed and how it is being assessed. They should be aware of their progress throughout their course of studies.

What I can tackle

The wider problem provides a more important, indeed essential 'improvement opportunity'. It is impossible to separate good assessment from effective teaching and learning. Any staff development activity must highlight the interrelation of each to the other. It would start with an analysis of teaching objectives and learning outcomes and then move on to consider how these might be assessed appropriately. Whereas *discrimination* or *bunching* would be addressed as an issue, it would not be the main theme. However, if good assessment policies and practices are developed and followed by all staff then it should be possible to defend the results of any assessment of student ability, including the distribution of classifications.

The main issues and modes of assessment include consideration of:

- The validity of the assessment procedures

- The reliability of the assessment procedures

- Setting clear criteria for assessment

- Enabling student learning and demonstration through assessment

- Using a variety of appropriate assessment methods

- Formative and summative assessment

- Continuous and terminal assessment

- Assessing product and process

- Criterion referenced and norm referenced assessment

- Coursework and examination

- Convergent and divergent assessment

Each course committee, module team and individual member of staff must consider an assessment strategy which is appropriate to the objectives of the element they are teaching. In particular, within level D [that is to say final year] modules at least, assessment should enable students to demonstrate their ability in the subject. This should not be done through the 'sting in the tail' approach which represents an implicit attempt to trap or trick the student, but rather through an understanding of the hierarchy of the cognitive domain demonstrated in the table below [Table 7.1]. Assessment should be divergent and allow the student to demonstrate her high level cognitive skills.

Although I chose to use Bloom's taxonomy (1956), it is not without its critics and I recognize that rival accounts are available. However, at this stage the important thing was to use a simple model to direct colleagues' attention to the importance of thinking about progression in learning in higher education. The paper continued as follows.

The role of Staff Development in tackling the problem

Of course, all of the issues outlined above need to be unpacked, and that unpacking goes beyond the scope of this paper.

But the real challenge is to engage every single member of academic staff in the exercise and in the practice of good assessment.

The objectives of the engagement are:

Table 7.1   *The hierarchy of the cognitive domain following Bloom's taxonomy (1956)*

Cognitive process	Explanation
Evaluation	Ability to make a judgement on the worth of something
Synthesis	Ability to combine separate elements into a whole
Analysis	Ability to break a problem into its constituent parts and establish the relationship between each one
Application	Ability to apply rephrased knowledge in a novel situation
Manipulation	Ability to rephrase knowledge
Knowledge	That which can be recalled

- To develop generic guidelines on good assessment
- To use these to design a good practice booklet on assessment for each faculty
- To evaluate these documents at departmental level and to adopt quality assessment practices within each course and each module delivered by the department.

The proposed programme

There would be six phases to the process:

Table 7.2   *The six phases of the programme. Progress from one phase to the next involves a movement of responsibility, and thus ownership, away from the ASDO to the academic staff.*

Phase	Actions
1. Raise awareness of the issue, create a need	Report (including statistics) to Deans, HoDs and academic staff; public lectures on new directions in assessment and on developing the independent learner
2. Working group to develop generic guidelines	Leader = academic staff development officer (ASDO), plus one senior representative from each faculty. Half-day preparation seminar led by external consultant
3. Faculty assessment team to design good assessment practice booklet	Leader = faculty rep from second phase plus two other faculty staff plus ASDO as adviser
4. Departmental evaluation	All departmental staff, led by ASDO and one faculty rep. Workshop objectives = (a) course/departmental strategy for assessment (b) individual awareness and practice
5. Delivery of departmental working document to faculty	Department to nominate a senior member/working group to deliver
6. The next step(s)	May look at specific areas, such as project assessment, practical work, assessing group work

The underlying philosophies behind this process are:

● That departments and staff should feel that through being involved in this process they have some ownership of the outcomes

● That ideas should be worked through into practice.

The continuing process (phase 6)

Discussions at all levels on bunching of marks so far have focused on the role of assessment. Indeed this paper, despite an early reference to the interrelation between assessment and teaching/learning, has also focused mainly on assessment alone; but we must start somewhere. However, I said earlier that a more fundamental approach should consider *at least* all aspects of assessment.

There is one other crucial factor which is involved in the problem, namely the early recognition of potential. An issue stated earlier compared formative and summative assessment. A related issue is the comparison between diagnosis and prediction. Rather than 'teaching to the middle', good assessment can be used to identify potential excellence as well as failure and should be an early step in the process of enabling a student to achieve his or her fullest potential. An awareness of this issue needs to be raised from the very beginning of a student's career in the university.

If our concern is to improve the honours classification statistics of the university without artificially manufacturing first class honours degrees, then we should be deeply concerned with developing the teaching quality of our staff. They are being bombarded with an ever increasing range of teaching initiatives and evaluations, but are not being given the resources to cope properly and professionally with these challenges.

The cost of the programme

This section of the presentation covered two aspects of cost. We start with Table 7.3.

On this basis the project was costed at 946 working days for the university, not including Staff Development planning and administration. Set against an annual load of 562,500 (2,500 staff working for 45 weeks), this gave a cost of 0.14 per cent of total staff time (or 0.49 per cent of *academic staff* time). This effectively demonstrated that, although this would be a significant project, it represented only a small commitment on the part of the university.

Table 7.3 *An estimate of the programme's cost in time*

People involved	Time cost of their actions
For each Head of Department	To allocate one departmental meeting to the exercise ($\frac{1}{2}$ day)
For each member of academic staff	$\frac{1}{2}$ day plus departmental meeting (1 day)
For each faculty representative	$1\frac{1}{2}$ days delivery (average) plus $1\frac{1}{2}$ days development (3 days)
For each team leader	3 days as Faculty rep plus 2 days development (5 days)
For the Academic Staff Development Officer	37 days delivery plus 2 days with team leaders plus 10 days with Faculty reps (49 days)

Support material

The final section of the paper provided a selection of good practices in assessment, collated from my own research into innovative teaching in higher education.

The outcome

The paper and its recommendations were accepted in their entirety by the committee. A summary of the proposals was presented to the university's policy and planning committee where the approval was endorsed and a recommendation made that attendance on the work-shops should be made compulsory for all academic staff.

Progress so far

The Deans nominated faculty representatives for the first stage of the programme, which began with a series of workshops in April 1994. These workshops were designed to meet three objectives:

● to identify the major issues to be addressed in the university's dis-cussion document

● to gather together good assessment practices from the faculties

● to determine the structure and outline for the document.

These objectives have essentially been met and work is progressing on the drafting of the document. It is intended that it will be completed by December 1994 and distributed to all academic staff by the end of January 1995.

The next phase will then be for the faculty representatives to form their own faculty working groups to produce faculty guidelines on effective assessment. These documents will build on two resources, namely the university discussion document and on the good practices identified within the faculties. The target date for completion of this phase is Easter 1995 and workshops for each School will begin soon after that date.

An outline grid for the university discussion document on assessment is given in Figure 7.3.

Table 7.4 identifies the main issues for inclusion in the university document on assessment.

Many examples of good practice have been gathered by the working group and will be used in either the discussion document or the Faculty guidelines. An outline of one example of good practice from the Department of Nursing is shown in Figure 7.4.

CONCLUSION

I began by saying that Staff and Educational Development are about change. In this chapter, I have identified some of the many features of a potential programme which staff and educational developers must analyse before determining what priority (if any) it should be given.

The case study identifies a potential project for staff and educational developers within one institution which meets many of the essential

	Issues	Advice	Examples
Level of action			
University			
Course or department			
Individual or module			

Figure 7.3   *The structure of the university discussion document*

Table 7.4   *A representation of the relationship between levels of decision making and assessment issues*

The level	The issues
University	<ul><li>Discriminating – stretching of marks</li><li>The use of information technology</li><li>Policy – examination boards; external examiners; procedures for progress, etc.</li><li>Course validation – appropriateness of assessment methods; cognitive levels; skills, outcomes and competences</li></ul>
Course or department	<ul><li>Assessment policy – role of assessment in course design; course/module assessment; balance between coursework and examinations; scheduling the assessments for each year</li><li>Quality assurance – standardizing criteria and marking schemes; norm or criterion referencing (pass/fail)</li><li>Assessment for learning – developing deep learning; assessing cognitive levels; developing independence</li><li>Quality enhancement – the role of staff and educational development</li></ul>
Individual or module	<ul><li>Assessment schedule</li><li>Validity against objectives</li><li>Individual practice – asking the right questions; criteria, advice and marking schemes; reliability; process and product; formative and summative; closed and open feedback; assignment attachment forms; self- and peer-assessment; group work</li></ul>

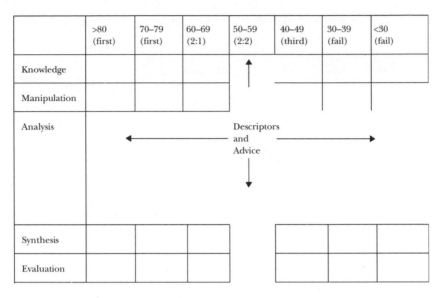

	>80 (first)	70–79 (first)	60–69 (2:1)	50–59 (2:2)	40–49 (third)	30–39 (fail)	<30 (fail)
Knowledge							
Manipulation							
Analysis				Descriptors and Advice			
Synthesis							
Evaluation							

Figure 7.4   *An example of an assessment grid showing how demonstration of cognitive levels maps to degree classifications. The boxes would contain descriptions of what should be found under a specific cognitive level for a student of a given ability*

criteria for a high-priority project (see Figure 7.1, page 97). This project meets these criteria. So, in respect of needs analysis:

● it is within the terms of reference of the unit

● it meets several institutional goals

● it has the approval and support of the Deans

● it reflects student concerns.

The priority given to the programme was based on the following assessment:

Impact

● it will engage every member of academic staff in the university

● it will directly affect the curriculum.

Resources

● a significant training programme has been established

- support will be provided by the Educational Development Unit
- the institution recognizes the magnitude of the project and the resources required

Motivation

- many staff recognize the need to change assessment procedures and practices
- many other staff feel they need help with their perceived problems with assessing their students.

Long-term benefits

- the programme will lead to changes in course design
- this will establish a long-term change
- staff will be better informed to continue to improve their assessment practices.

It is important to recognize these features of a potential high-priority development programme and to be sufficiently flexible to be able to act quickly and effectively in response to this recognition.

Finally, this case study has shown that assessment reform cannot be considered in isolation from a review of teaching and learning practices.

Chapter 8

Embedding Alternative Approaches in Assessment

Hazel Fullerton

This chapter follows the development and integration of alternative approaches to assessment through a change agent cascade programme at the University of Plymouth. No claims are made for the uniqueness of the alternatives. What is unique, is that the process of their introduction, adaptation, implementation, dissemination and widespread adoption can be tracked. Some of these mechanisms include a series of posters of the innovations which are presented in this chapter as figures and the context and process are discussed.

CHANGING PRACTICE

As the prospect of greatly increased numbers of students became a reality, three problems which concerned us most were: 'How to maintain personal contact with students?', 'How to improve students' learning?', and 'How to cope with assessment?' Our response was to devise a cascade programme to focus on each of these concerns, comprising a group of 18 change agents for each concern. Theirs was to be a crucial role and they were selected on the basis of their openness to new ideas and their credibility with their colleagues.

Each focus area had its own programme, the support of internal and external experts, and study materials. Two days of input was available to each of the focus areas: one on dissemination design and a further three for study and dissemination itself. The high proportion of time on dissemination recognizes the difference between awareness raising and actually changing practice and the difficulty of moving from the former to the latter. Those sessions included the group identifying the potential threats to the process and their own fears. These were not illusory as the change agents were variously viewed as the tools of management and *agents provocateurs.*

111

An important feature was that the change agents were paid for their participation. While many of them insisted that they would have done it without the money, it did lend a certain kudos and seriousness to the work. Payment was against the allocated hours, at the part-time lecturers' rate. It was not 'hard currency' but an account which could be used by these change agents to order whatever they wished to help them in their work – generally equipment, software, or conferences fees. One interesting interpretation of this was a round table. The person concerned felt his rectangular desk was limiting 'sharing and owning' in meetings. He proceeded to set up quality circles around his round table and subsequently led the department to an 'excellent' rating.

FOCUS ON ASSESSMENT

Of all the focus areas, assessment was regarded as the most pressing. While lecturers can usually handle four times as many students in a lecture, marking of 250 scripts is another matter entirely. Alternatives had to be found. The group adopted the notion of 'Working smarter not harder' (see Figure 8.1), but tempered it with an initial consensus that techniques would only be considered if they were also in the interests of students' learning. For many this proved a significant phase in their appreciation of the interdependence of assessment/curriculum/learning.

Working smarter not harder

The poster shown as Figure 8.1 was produced by a sub-group shortly after the input days. It was devised as a form of framework onto which alternatives could be plotted and to help the change agents to investigate where relative benefits might be had. Central to this framework is the crucial role of questioning what is being done and why.

There are both vertical and horizontal axes for 'smarter' and 'harder'. To the left these are considered from the point of view of the benefit to the student, increasing their autonomy and ability to monitor their own learning. On the right they are viewed from the lecturers' perspective and the potential for monitoring students' learning. The top and bottom quadrants of the square reflect the balance between extrinsic (external expectations) and intrinsic (students' wanting to learn) motivations as they relate to assessment. The group also referred to that valuable external motivation which assessment provides, ie, 'make the buggers work'.

Note that amongst the examples around the square, 'MCQs' (multiple-

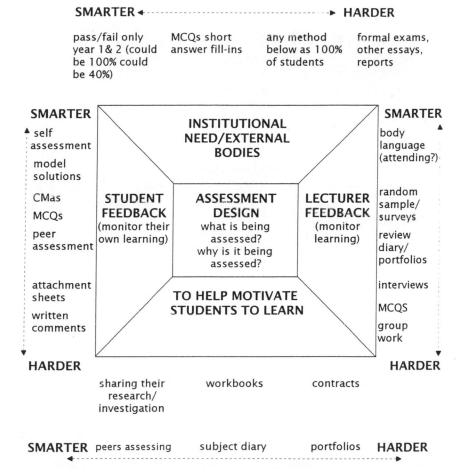

SMARTER ←·····················→ HARDER

| pass/fail only year 1& 2 (could be 100% could be 40%) | MCQs short answer fill-ins | any method below as 100% of students | formal exams, other essays, reports |

SMARTER
- self assessment
- model solutions
- CMas
- MCQs
- peer assessment
- attachment sheets
- written comments
HARDER

INSTITUTIONAL NEED/EXTERNAL BODIES

STUDENT FEEDBACK (monitor their own learning)

ASSESSMENT DESIGN
what is being assessed?
why is it being assessed?

LECTURER FEEDBACK (monitor learning)

TO HELP MOTIVATE STUDENTS TO LEARN

SMARTER
- body language (attending?)
- random sample/ surveys
- review diary/ portfolios
- interviews
- MCQS
- group work
HARDER

| sharing their research/ investigation | workbooks | contracts |

SMARTER peers assessing   subject diary   portfolios HARDER
←·····················→

Figure 8.1 *Working smarter, not harder*

choice tests) appears closer to the 'smarter' end of the spectrum for students than it does on the lecturers' side. This reflects the hard work needed by academic staff wanting to initiate a good question bank (see Figure 8.5 for a poster illustrating a way of helping to compile questions).

The idea of introducing 'pass/fail' beyond first-year modules has not yet gone very far but there was a minority of change agents who pressed the management to abandon the classified degree system.

Apart from that, all the ideas here have been refined and are in current use. Even the 'harder' alternatives such as portfolios are now fairly common because of their contribution to the student's growing autonomy.

EMBEDDING ALTERNATIVE PRACTICE

The dissemination was devised by each faculty's change agents meeting to plan their approach. The majority of these meetings were 'away days' and some change agents invited others from different faculties to join their away days. This cross-fertilization also continues.

The away days produced a number of 'champions' and 'early adopters', people who identified approaches appropriate to their subject and way of working. Meanwhile, other changes, such as modularization and semesterization, were emerging. Sessions for module leaders were organized to embed further the home-grown alternatives that the change agents had seeded. Posters were created to illustrate the alternatives and developed as the gist of innovative ideas was gathered from each change agent by phone. The key points were organized, word-processed onto A4, drawings were added and then photocopied for use in an A1-size poster, and then layout and colour were done by hand.

THE POSTER SESSIONS

The posters were hung around a room in groups, accompanied by related notes or examples of practices referred to in the posters. The module leaders browsed through these to grasp some of the range, scope and different angles represented.

Each originator then had five minutes to explain briefly the solution represented by their poster and the associated process. Questions were then written on 'post-its' which were stuck on to specific posters and to which the 'owner' responded. Module leaders used sticky dots to indicate points they wanted to explore further and small groups were formed with the innovator/owner joining the group to act as consultant to help them devise appropriate variations and applications.

The following posters, shown in Figures 8.2–8.4 are not all original and you may recognize some – or at least their close cousins. However, many are now used widely in the institution, none was being used prior to the cascade programme and each has since established its own identity and place in its curriculum.

Doing it in class

Civil engineering students working on projects were spending disproportionate amounts of time on the gloss of laser printing and fancy binding which often obscured the thinking processes that the tutors wanted to observe. Increasing group sizes also limited the amount of tutor feedback.

- in groups of 3 and 4 (64 in cohort)
- against the clock
- mirrors industrial practice
- focuses on quality not quantity

PROCESS	GROUP	LECTURER
Session 1 *1 hour*	brief to all teams of 3 or 4 come up with 3 proposal solutions	lecturer marks & selects one
Session 2 *2 hours*	team asked for specific information & costing's related to chosen solution	lecturer comments
Session 3 *1 hour*	team responds to comments etc	
Session 4 *2 hours*	hands in completed work	lecturer gives final summative mark

advantages

- *stops students spending unnecessary time on minor projects*
- *develops cooperative team work skills*
- *allows student to demonstrate what they CAN do*
- *students can reference each other's work, consult lecturers and other sources of information NB final exam is open book*

Figure 8.2 *Doing it in class*

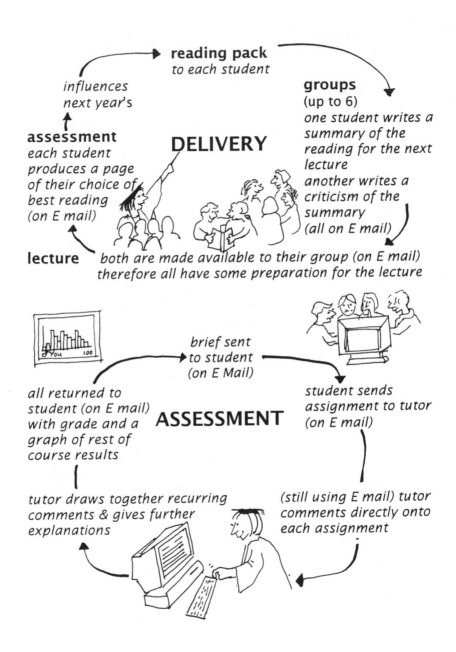

reading pack
to each student

influences
next year's

groups
(up to 6)
one student writes a
summary of the
reading for the next
lecture
another writes a
criticism of the
summary
(all on E mail)

assessment
each student
produces a page
of their choice of
best reading
(on E mail)

DELIVERY

lecture   both are made available to their group (on E mail)
therefore all have some preparation for the lecture

brief sent
to student
(on E Mail)

all returned to
student (on E mail)
with grade and a
graph of rest of
course results

ASSESSMENT

student sends
assignment to tutor
(on E mail)

tutor draws together recurring
comments & gives further
explanations

(still using E mail) tutor
comments directly onto
each assignment

Figure 8.3   *Using E-mail in course delivery and in assessment*

AIMS
reduce lecturer marking load

maintain levels of student
assessment
(formative & summative)

METHOD
**LECTURER MARKS SAMPLE OF
QUESTIONS** *(summative)*

set 10 problems & mark 3

request full student solutions
to all questions

STUDENT MARKS THE REST
using detailed solutions
provided by lecturer *(formative)*

RESULTS   **STUDENT NUMBERS UP
WORKLOAD DOWN**

Figure 8.4   *Proportionate marking*

The first strategy introduced group projects, which meant that 25 group projects were produced annually instead of over 80 individual projects. This also involved teamwork – a crucial skill for professionals in this discipline. The second strategy was to do the projects in class, against the clock, so notes, etc. had to be very well organized if they were to be effectively accessible within the constrained timescale. The formative tutor feedback between stages simulated real-world interaction between the client and other related professionals.

The students have to divide the work up amongst the group but each student's name appears on the sheets that he/she has worked on, so the tutor can tell who did what. The project comes in, 'warts and all' and the tutor can trace the development of the group's thinking, calculations, dead ends and such like. As a result, feedback can be targeted more closely to where it will really help.

Although a group project takes longer to mark than an individual one, better quality feedback is possible and, even then, overall marking time is reduced by over 50 per cent. Throughout the project, the working processes and atmosphere are far more professionally relevant and there is a more organic relationship between the students' working and learning.

The tutor now uses a similar approach in a three-hour, in-class, open-book, end-of-module examination.

Integrating computer network in assessment

One of the objectives on this business studies course is to make students conversant and comfortable with communicating through computer-based technologies. As this is done both in the delivery and the assessment of the module, both are described here.

The delivery is through a reading pack and traditional lectures. For each lecture, two students within each small learning group do the preparatory work for the rest of their group. Both have to work through the readings in the pack for the next lecture; one to write a summary of it, the other to write a criticism of that summary. Before the lecture, the summary and criticisms are made available to the rest of the group at their shared E-mail address, so all are prepared for the lecture. This organization of the reading exercises encourage reading before lectures and allow the tutor to monitor the process by reviewing the E-mail activity.

As well as a traditional assessment, there is an end-of-course assignment that requires that each student should choose the reading she or he considers to be the best from the pack and then produce an E-mail page explaining and justifying his or her choice. This helps the lecturer to understand how the readings are perceived by the group and in turn influences the composition of the reading pack in subsequent years.

What the student then gets back on E-mail is her or his own feedback and information relating to the other readings produced by the rest of the cohort.

This innovation was devised some years ago but has fresh implications now that our residences have networked computers and more students living at a distance have computers with E-mail facilities.

Proportionate marking

Irritated by students doing insufficient work between sessions to consolidate their learning, with the result that they were scarcely able to build onto it in the following session, a maths lecturer introduced weekly, marked exercises. Then the numbers rose from 20 to 80! In order to survive he devised a simple, alternative strategy.

He now sets ten questions each week but only marks three. He doesn't decide which three to mark until he sits down with the pile of answers, so he can't 'give it away'. Then he chooses three which will check their fundamental grasp of the key concepts. The other seven questions are self-assessed by the students, using full solutions with explanatory steps which he subsequently supplies.

The system provides both formative and summative assessment and encourages students to be involved fully in their own learning. The tutor-marked elements lead to a summative grading. The student-marked problems provide sufficient practice to test students' understanding. Maths students, who understand the law of averages, realize that trying to claim that they 'did better on the student-marked ones' is a fruitless pursuit.

Although more up-front work is involved for the tutor in producing the worked examples, this is more than offset by the reduction in marking time. The students are actually more involved. Previously, tutor marks had been accepted passively with little attempt to explore the solutions.

FURTHER USES OF THE POSTERS

The posters have been used with Certificate of Education groups, with our new lecturers' course, with a postgraduate module on assessment and at the May 1994 SEDA conference.

After browsing, participants select which posters they want to know more about and the originators offer the necessary explanations. Then pairs of participants share their own good ideas on assessment. Some will volunteer to explain their ideas to the larger group. A rough poster of an idea, technique or approach is drawn up while it is being explained and this is tidied up on the computer later. If useful, it's enlarged and added to the collection. 'Question bank', shown in Figure 8.5, is an example of a good idea generated in this way at the SEDA conference. It was originated and volunteered by Professor Phil Race.

Question bank

In this each student has to produce 300 questions, which benefits both the lecturer and the student. The lecturer gains literally hundreds of questions – a rich vein for possible multiple-choice tests. The students need to have a broad understanding of the underlying principles and their applicability across the sciences. As any teacher knows, it's not until you teach and try to assess something that you get to the heart of the matter. There is an interesting cycle in which the assignment is the revision of the course, which in turn forms the preparation for the assignment. The students are learning better through their involvement with the materials and through reviewing and interacting with their knowledge. They have to go back over all the work distinguishing the key points from the trivial, which involves categorization that leads to seeing connections between modules. In order to meet the 'one-liner' criterion, they have to break concepts down into their constituent elements.

It motivates revision because it is fun and a challenge. Obviously with 300 questions to be produced they won't all be brilliantly original but equally obviously they have to reflect the whole field of study. This is, then, a tool for revision that encourages students to use it to revise with each other, thus explaining the material to each other and further consolidating their learning. A particular value of this is the way that the allocation of 10 per cent of the marks for the design tool (the form in which the questions are presented) engages and values the student's creativity and imagination. The more they are engaged at this level, the deeper the involvement and better the learning.

WHAT IS NOW EMBEDDED?

Generally there is evidence of a much greater variety of approaches to assessment being used. There is a better match of assessment process to the objectives being tested, so that,

- multiple-choice questionnaires are used to assess factual knowledge and numeric elements
- assertion/reason tests, in objective-response format, are used to

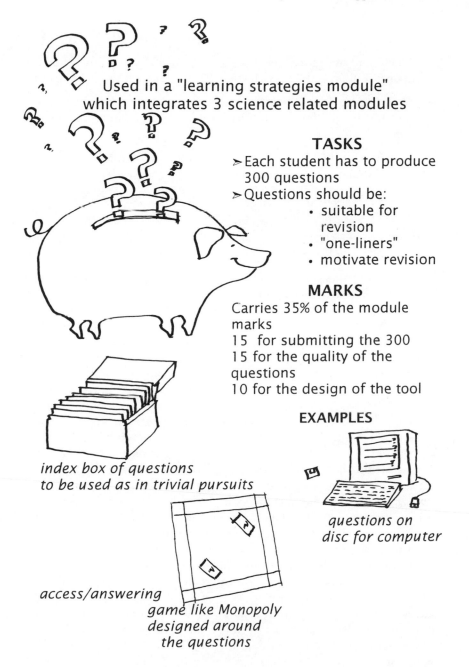

Used in a "learning strategies module"
which integrates 3 science related modules

TASKS
➤ Each student has to produce 300 questions
➤ Questions should be:
  - suitable for revision
  - "one-liners"
  - motivate revision

MARKS
Carries 35% of the module marks
15 for submitting the 300
15 for the quality of the questions
10 for the design of the tool

EXAMPLES

index box of questions to be used as in trivial pursuits

questions on disc for computer

access/answering game like Monopoly designed around the questions

Figure 8.5 *Question bank*

determine grasp of concepts. These objective tests are marked by optical mark readers (OMRs)

- attachment sheets are very widely used to speed turn-around time and to ensure that students get feedback on an agreed range of criteria

- 'front-ending' is now more common, with better module descriptions and better briefing, and discussion and negotiation of relevant criteria

- self-assessment is now more common and is valued for its formative role in students' personal development

- peer-assessment of group projects and presentations fosters and recognizes transferable skills

- portfolios and learning logs are used to allow individual exploration and reflective learning.

There are, of course, associated concerns with all of these. There is a risk of overuse of a particular technique, as when one faculty realized that too high a proportion of some students' marks was based on peer-assessment, which is now limited to 45 per cent of the total marks available. Similarly, although good objective tests are hard to devise initially, the processing through OMRs is fast, easy and is so amenable to a variety of analysis that this process is very seductive and could lead to an unhealthy balance of assessing memory rather than higher order cognitive skills. We have also noted that the distribution of marks has changed in the wake of this assessment reform, which may be a cause for concern amongst those who felt that the earlier distribution was the right distribution.

Even in the early adopters' departments, not all were convinced. Then a curious thing happened. In one faculty, students started to put pressure on the unconverted: 'So-and-so does it this way and it's much better/ fairer/more interesting'. That Dean played his role well, not imposing but participating in away days, listening and supporting. A 'critical mass' was built up and this has led to more recalcitrant staff being pulled along in its wake.

Of course there were also other initiatives involved, for example EHE was crucial in supporting further investigation and development of some of the innovations. But, reflecting upon the process, it is clear that adversity in the form of increased student numbers and structural changes actually helped to kick the whole process into gear. Change would have been much harder to initiate if it had been feasible to maintain the status quo, but that was no longer an option.

The cascade did work well. It was a 'bottom up' initiative from an *ad hoc* group of concerned staff. To some extent it was also dependent on strong backing from the Chancellory who were forthcoming with the finance to support and recognize the effort of change agents. The effectiveness of the process is not lost on Higher Education Quality Council and Higher Education Funding Council for England auditors and assessors.

The change agent process in itself is now embedded and its current focus is on flexible learning.

Chapter 9

When Tutors Assess: Who Can Help and How?

Kate Day and Dai Hounsell

INTRODUCTION

Over the last decade in particular, universities have increasingly recognized the need for and the benefits of systematic training and development – at least in relation to their mainstream teaching staff. Thus an array of induction courses and update events, run for the most part by central educational or staff development units in cooperation with academic colleagues, now provide opportunities for lecturers to enhance their knowledge, understanding, confidence and competence concerning the processes and practicalities of learning, teaching and assessment. It is only much more recently that the spotlight has begun to pick out a less visible and more transient component of the university teaching workforce: the part-time tutors, language assistants and laboratory demonstrators who are being increasingly deployed – especially in universities with a high research profile – as a way of squaring the circle of larger student classes combined with tight constraints on resources. For, despite a long history of the casual employment of postgraduates and others in these teaching support roles in many UK universities, there are no well-established training and development strategies for this particular group on a par with those widely found in North American universities and colleges where the use of graduate 'teaching assistants' is commonplace. However, the recent rapid rise in Britain in the use of part-time tutors, allied to understandable concerns not to put teaching quality in jeopardy as a consequence, have prompted question as to what kinds of training and development this group ought to be offered – and indeed required to undertake.

In this chapter we want to consider how those part-time tutors who are involved in some aspect of the assessment process can be helped to perform their duties in ways that are demonstrably fair, efficient and effective, from the viewpoints of the tutors, students and departments concerned. Our discussion will draw in particular on recent experiences and developments at the University of Edinburgh, where the Centre for Teaching, Learning and Assessment (TLA Centre), working in close conjunction with departments and faculties, has well-established training programmes for incoming lecturers and laboratory demonstrators. It also mounts both regular and occasional training events for those teaching staff with specialized roles and responsibilities, such as course organizers, postgraduate supervisors, and directors of studies (that is to say, designated academic and personal advisers to students). Over the past few years, and assisted recently by two externally funded projects, the TLA Centre has been actively engaged in developing specific training opportunities while at the same time generally encouraging the more satisfactory and systematic provision of briefing, training and support for postgraduate and other part-time tutors.

ASSESSMENT AND PART-TIME TUTORING

Assessment is a critical focus of attention in any programme for university teachers, not simply because of the considerable time and effort it demands, but also because of the dilemmas it poses in trying to reconcile the tensions between the summative purposes of assessment-for-grading and the formative purposes of assessment-for-learning (Hounsell and Murray, 1992). A closely related consideration is the potentially powerful impact of the tasks set, the judgements made, and the feedback given, on what students learn and on how they go about their learning. Yet acknowledging the centrality of assessment tends to be a more straightforward matter than determining what training methods and activities will most help university teachers come to grips with its exacting demands and challenges. Regulations and procedures often operate at several institutional levels, and there are the technicalities of different types of assessment, of scaling and of aggregating marks or grades. Moreover, there are substantial variations between different disciplines and departments in the criteria for grading that are likely to be seen as the most appropriate. Likewise, considerable differences exist in the course contexts within which productive feedback strategies are to be devised and implemented. The challenge of assessment is all the greater, however, when the training and development are being targeted not at established, mainstream lecturers but at the growing number of postgraduate and other part-time tutors whose devolved responsibilities extend to some aspects of assessment.

Part-time tutors, it is often remarked, are generally highly committed to their students, as well as greatly valued by their institutional colleagues.

Nevertheless, many of the characteristic features of part-time tutors may render their training and development problematic, both in general terms and as regards assessment. They are a short-term workforce with only partial teaching responsibilities; a temporary group of largely transient 'birds of passage', as a survey conducted at Edinburgh in 1993 clearly demonstrated (Knottenbelt and Fiddes, 1994). The survey, which was undertaken as part of a project funded initially by the Universities' Funding Council and subsequently by the Scottish Higher Education Funding Council (SHEFC), encompassed the two-thirds of the University's departments which made use of part-time tutors and which together employed more than 550 individuals. It indicated that although some individuals had worked on a casually paid basis for ten or 12 years, most people undertook tutorial teaching for between one-and-a-half and three years. In addition to the repeated training demands, generated by a relatively fast turnover rate, part-time tutors' backgrounds and prior experience have tended to be quite diverse, making it hard to establish common starting points. Even in Edinburgh's case, with its strong research tradition and large pool of research students, postgraduates were slightly outnumbered by other kinds of part-time tutors, who included graduate professionals, early- or semi- retired academics and postdoctoral fellows.

Also variable – and not necessarily always clearly defined – were the duties for which part-time tutors need preparing. Formal commitments can range from two or three one-off seminars, through an honours class on topics of specialist interest and knowledge, to regular weekly first- or second-year tutorials covering broad subject areas: all in all a pattern of commitment much more diverse than that which underpins recent proposals for tutor training (Elton *et al.*, 1994). But there were also other influential sources of variation. Group sizes mostly cluster in the ten to 20 range but sometimes substantially larger numbers of students are involved; while the practical roles that tutors are called upon to play in different courses are inevitably strongly shaped by departmental cultures and requirements of a very localized kind (Becher, 1989). Indeed, the Edinburgh survey reported considerable variations in the extent to which postgraduate and other part-time tutors were responsible for deciding what and how to teach, designing tutorial materials, assigning preparation tasks, and being involved in the assessment of students' learning. No less importantly, many part-time tutors were constrained by a lack of access to the same kind of institutional base, communication facilities and other resources that established lecturers normally have – and perhaps too readily take for granted. This has implications for tutoring practice, but is understandable given that tutors' primary allegiances lie elsewhere; for postgraduates with their thesis research and for other people, with their external commitments. Given their semi-detached position, part-time tutors can only be expected to have a 'pinhole' view of what goes on, of how things work, and of how their own tutoring activities fit with the wider picture that obtains at course and departmental levels. Clearly then there are both time and perceptual constraints which, taken together with what particular groups of tutors' contractual obligations specify and reward, will affect the scope that exists for training, while at the same time colouring tutors' attitudes and reactions to whatever they are offered.

ASSESSMENT TASKS AND ROLES

So far we have concentrated on the challenges presented for training and development by the combination of a problematic training area (assessment) and a problematic target group (part-time tutors). But it is important not to lose sight of the more limited range of functions within the assessment spectrum that part-time tutors – as compared to main-stream lecturers – tend to undertake.

Figure 9.1 illustrates the component tasks within the assessment role and, of the nine aspects listed, tutors involved in assessment are likely to be concerned with items 3, 4, and 5, somewhat with 7, possibly with 2, and rarely if ever with 1, 6, 8 and 9. In this respect the agenda for tutor training is rather more focused, and potentially more manageable, than when working with other teaching staff.

But it is also important not to concentrate solely on the training dimension in considering the question of, 'When tutors assess, who can help and how?' After all, many of the difficulties which the various stakeholders involved may encounter are not, it should be emphasized, purely and simply training matters. Problems arise, for example, for tutors if 'teaching' responsibilities include assessment without explicit remuneration; for students if tutors are not appropriately available for pre- or post-assignment guidance; and for institutions if the marking of assessed work by tutors is not properly supervised and would not readily satisfy quality assurance and other accountability requirements. So, when part-time tutors are involved in assessment, effective assistance is likely to be afforded as much by consideration and resolution of policy matters and by the provision of departmentally based briefing and support as it is by training alone. Accordingly, while this chapter's principal focus is the strategic planning and content of tutor training for assessment, the wider issues of institutional policy-making and departmental practice are also of direct concern.

Course Organizer or Lecturer	←——— Who Does What ...? ———→	Tutor
	1. CHOOSING ASSESSMENT METHODS (and deciding marks weightings)	
	2. DEVISING ASSIGNMENTS, TEST PAPERS, etc	
	3. GROUNDWORK (leading up to a particular assignment)	
	4. BRIEFING AND ADVISING STUDENTS	
	5. MARKING AND COMMENTING	
	6. VERIFYING AND VALIDATING MARKS	
	7. FOLLOWING-UP FEEDBACK	
	8. REVIEWING STUDENTS' PERFORMANCE (for the course as a whole)	
	9. REVIEWING ASSESSMENT OUTCOMES (as part of course feedback and evaluation)	

Figure 9.1 *Who does what?*

A WORKSHOP PROGRAMME

Against this background we now turn to the workshops on assessment that we have been running for postgraduate tutors, and in particular to the sessions geared towards tutors drawn from the faculty group of arts, divinity and music who are required to mark and provide feedback on coursework essays. The group of tutors concerned were postgraduates selected as 'teaching award holders' under a scheme whereby a flat fee was offered in addition to payment per tutorial and in which participation in quite an intensive training programme was compulsory. The training provided formed part of a larger orientation programme, developed with the financial support of the SHEFC.

Both the format and the content of the assessment workshops, which occupied two, late afternoon one-and-a-half hour slots, were the outgrowth of the planning, feedback and reworking cycle engaged in during two runnings of an earlier series of workshops. Short scene-setting or information-giving inputs from us as convenors were combined with individual reflection and small group discussion, focusing on four sequential themes (shown in Figure 9.2):

● groundwork

● briefing and advising students

● marking and commenting

● review and follow-up.

Drawing on their experiences as undergraduates, and as tutors for those not new to the job, participants were encouraged to identify a repertoire of possible strategies likely to prove both practicable (for tutors) and productive (for students). Since we were not in a position to engage with the content- and context-specific elements of individual tutors' assessment tasks, our principal contribution, in collaboration with our colleague Charles Anderson, was to chart the assessment process by means of an organizing framework and to pinpoint the various demands entailed. This systematic overview, reproduced on a smaller scale as Figure 9.2, aimed to set boundaries and so to clarify what is entailed in assessment for part-time tutors and to alert them to what they would need to know or find out. Procedurally, the framework also served to signal the shape and substance of the sessions, while the sub-headings with their illustrative examples (and deliberate blank spaces) provided a basis for generating and locating ideas about how best to approach and set about assessment.

In courses for other groups of part-time tutors we have taken a similar

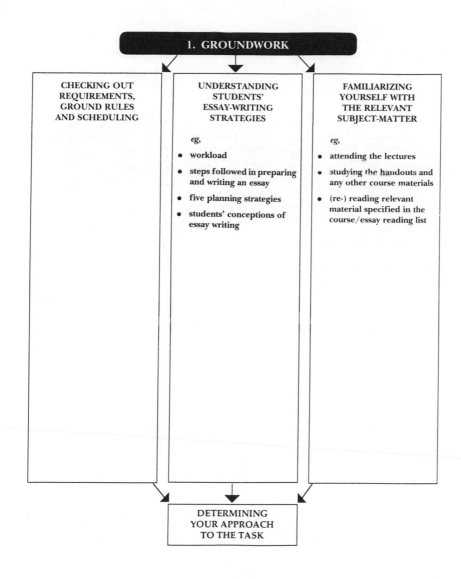

1. GROUNDWORK

CHECKING OUT REQUIREMENTS, GROUND RULES AND SCHEDULING	UNDERSTANDING STUDENTS' ESSAY-WRITING STRATEGIES	FAMILIARIZING YOURSELF WITH THE RELEVANT SUBJECT-MATTER
	eg,	*eg,*
	• workload	• attending the lectures
	• steps followed in preparing and writing an essay	• studying the handouts and any other course materials
	• five planning strategies	• (re-) reading relevant material specified in the course/essay reading list
	• students' conceptions of essay writing	

DETERMINING YOUR APPROACH TO THE TASK

Figure 9.2 *Assessment, marking and feedback: coursework essays*

2. BRIEFING AND ADVISING STUDENTS

CLARIFYING WHAT?	BRIEFING HOW?	ADVISING WHEN?
eg,	*eg,*	*eg,*
• requirements (scope, length, format)	• course/departmental handbook	• at start of course/term
• ground-rules (use of (re)sources, bibliographic presentation)	• handouts	• when the essay is assigned
• marking criteria	• tutorial time	• once students have embarked on their essays
• scheduling	• by recommending study guides/faculty workshops	
• appropriate essay-writing strategies	• one-to-one consultation	
• any queries students raise		

Figure 9.2 *(Continued)*

3. MARKING AND COMMENTING

MARKING THE ESSAYS

eg.

- sampling and surveying
- reading and marking, with reference to the assessment criteria and/or marking scheme
- reviewing marks across the range

ESSAY COMMENTS

... on what? eg,

- content
- structure
- style and presentation
- grammar and punctuation
- other assessment criteria
- moving forward: prioritizing

... how? eg,

- open
- focused
- proformas

CONSULTING WITH REFERRAL TO COURSE ORGANIZER/MENTOR

eg,

- as a check on marking standards
- as a check on quantity and quality of written comments

KEEPING METICULOUS RECORDS

4. REVIEW AND FOLLOW-UP

TO THE GROUP AS A WHOLE

eg,

- class pointers
- referring back to earlier advice

TO INDIVIDUAL STUDENTS

eg,

- one-to-one guidance
- referring back to earlier marks and comments

Figure 9.2 *(Continued)*

kind of approach to training for assessment, though in the activities open to postgraduate and part-time tutors throughout the university, for example, assessment is the subject of one of the follow-up seminars rather than part of the introductory orientation day. Wherever possible the TLA Centre has also encouraged more locally-based training efforts by running, for example, a pilot 'tutoring the tutors' seminar for course organizers and by contributing to faculty- or departmentally-run events. Whatever particular form the workshops have taken, they have been nested within a strategic view of face-to-face training as only one of several ways in which tutors could be helped to carry out their assessment and other responsibilities. The SHEFC-funded orientation programme, for example, has both an associated mentoring scheme and specially developed written resource materials to provide additional guidance and support. In *Tutoring. A Handbook for Postgraduate and Other Part-time Tutors* (Forster and Hounsell, 1994), the faculty group's setting out of 'Roles and Responsibilities' is followed by chapters from TLA contributors concerned with 'Preparing and Conducting Tutorials', 'Student Learning', 'Supporting and Advising Students', 'Working with Others', 'Feedback on Tutoring' and 'Taking Things Forward', as well as the chapter on 'Coursework Assessment and Feedback'. The benefits of the close involvement of academic staff from the faculty group, whether in planning and running workshops, acting as mentors to the award holders, or commenting on drafts of the *Handbook*, have confirmed our initial instinct that it was vital that those seeking to offer assistance to tutors should work as close as to the course-level ground as possible. Also reinforced is our belief in briefing and support as critical adjuncts to training and development. This is especially true as regards assessment, where it is essential that part-time tutors should have an informed and precise understanding of what is expected of them and their students, including the standards expected by particular courses within a discipline and the criteria by which assessed work is to be judged. Tutors need to know where assessment fits with the key objectives and substantive content of a particular course, as well as having opportunities to pick up and enhance the more generic notions and skills that can be fostered by more centralized training provision.

THE POLICY DIMENSION

Briefing, training and support, even if energetically and systematically offered in different ways and at local as well as other institutional levels, may not be sufficient to help tutors in the responsible and productive discharge of their assigned assessment duties. Our own institution is one of those that has come to recognize a need to tackle the policy dimension in order to ensure that postgraduate and other part-time tutors are able to do a good job. The 1993 university-wide survey at Edinburgh identified two rather different sets of concerns to which the devolution of marking to part-time tutors gave rise. The first set of worries might be particularly troublesome or problematic for some part-time tutors, but are the kind of challenges that tutors in general have to face. These included worries about how to handle and grade a large volume of scripts, prioritize and weight assessment criteria, or provide student feedback effectively yet economically – in other words, the sort of concerns that can be addressed during training sessions of various kinds and possibly, though not necessarily, resolved by the ideas and practical suggestions generated.

The other type of worry, expressed in at least some quarters, indicated a lack of sufficiently robust policy frameworks to achieve acceptable levels of good practice. Fears as to whether, for example, the marking function carried out by postgraduate and other part-time tutors was being sufficiently well supervised or properly remunerated can be understood within a general concern for the quality assurance and contractual issues for which institutions are held accountable. Accordingly, attention has now been focused not simply on training and development matters but also on making policy decisions and on improvements in procedures in the area of postgraduate and other part-time tutoring. The steps taken so far with regard to assessment involve all tutors having contracts or letters of appointment that include specification of any responsibilities for marking or otherwise assessing students' work. If responsibilities *do* include marking, commenting on and assessing students' coursework or examination papers, the course organizers concerned are obliged to ensure that the work assessed is subject to double-marking (meaning that the tutor's marking should be supervised and some sampling done). Meanwhile, a working party on part-time tutoring and demonstrating with a broad-ranging remit has been appointed, and is due to report on its policy recommendations before the close of the current academic year.

CONCLUDING COMMENTS

As indicated at the outset, many universities are currently deriving considerable benefits from employing postgraduate and part-time tutors, in terms of helping to cope with larger class sizes when resources are constrained, thereby affording some protection for an institution's research endeavours or giving students access to particular professional expertise. Tutors themselves commonly put a lot into working with their students, gaining both personal satisfaction and additional experience. However, their deployment also requires careful management, both centrally and locally, so that they are not exploited or expected to do the impossible, but are adequately briefed, trained, resourced and supported in their teaching functions – including assessment where appropriate. Institutions have to recognize that the level of investment required to ensure the delivery of good quality teaching and assessment is likely to be proportionately greater for tutors than for mainstream lecturers. Any new member of staff calls for 'capital' investment in initial training and briefing and 'recurrent' investment in on-going support and enhancement of expertise. But the turnover among tutors who are not departmentally embedded means that a succession of people are constantly having to go through a similar learning curve.

The job of briefing, training and support also needs to be a partnership, capitalizing on what central providers (educational development units or teaching and learning centres) can offer of a 'broad-brush' generic kind, but equally, and perhaps more crucially, drawing firmly on very localized inputs as regards training, and particularly in terms of briefing and support. Course induction, documentation and communication have a crucial part to play in assisting postgraduate and other part-time tutors. Yet, while giving due recognition to the high degree of particularity of tutors' teaching and assessment roles, it is also difficult to see how from the viewpoints of quality and accountability universities can avoid setting firm and explicit institution-wide boundaries on the role of tutors in assessment, and thus provide more robust policy and practical frameworks within which course and departmental tailoring can be constructively accommodated. We owe it to our students to ensure that their work is skilfully and reliably assessed, and even when assessment is undertaken by university teachers who are well qualified and experienced, the process still requires proper oversight and monitoring. We also owe it to ourselves as staff developers to pool institutional experiences and to learn from one another how best to meet the challenges of using part-time tutors and of helping them when they are involved in assessment.

Chapter 10

Assessing 'Seminar' Work: Students as Teachers

Phyllis Creme

Several years ago, after consultation with students and colleagues, the film studies staff group on the University of North London's humanities degree scheme adopted a different category for assessment on all units except the introductory one of the pathway: assessment of student's 'seminar' work. The purpose of this chapter is to explore the impact of this move on student learning. I will argue that changes in what is assessed have implications for how the assessment is carried out and, specifically, that this is a case where the introduction of peer- and self-assessment would be appropriate. I was then a part of the staff group but now I teach only on the occasional unit, from one of which the examples below are drawn.

Seminar groups of around 20 students, meeting usually on alternate weeks of the unit, are sub-divided into small groups of four to five, which each have to plan and organize a learning session for the whole group, commonly based on one film or extract. The students thus become 'teachers' (rather than, for instance, presenters of papers). They are assessed on their contribution to all the seminar sessions on the basis of teacher observations and their own written individual and group statements.

The assessment originally carried 10 per cent of the total for each unit but because of the success of the scheme this is now being increased to 20 per cent. Marks are allocated according to pre-specified, written criteria, which include reference to: 'regular attendance; preparation; listening; useful questioning; relevant argument'. In their written statements students are asked to comment on what they have contributed to and learned from the process.

REASONS FOR THE CHANGE

The main reason for this change in assessment was to give formal

137

acknowledgement to the importance of group work on the programme, both as a means of learning the subject and of acquiring transferable 'life' skills. Group discussion was not an 'extra' but a fundamental part of being a film student. There was also an equal opportunities dimension: some students were clearly performing more effectively in group, oral work than in their writing.

The fact that initially only 10 per cent of the total marks were allocated to this reflected a caution about the change, particularly on the part of students, which was expressed as a concern with difficulties in the reliability of the grading process. The written individual and group statements by students were intended to address that difficulty: they were a product the external examiner could see. On the other hand, they entailed reverting to using writing for assessment, more than was perhaps originally intended.

Regular evaluation of the units is carried out through questionnaires for each unit; the students' written statements; informal discussion with students; and considerable discussion among tutors. Issues that have arisen include: the impact on the relationship between tutors and students and between students and students; the use of resources; the role of the tutors; the difference that the increase from 10 per cent to 20 per cent will make; and appropriate ways to carry out the assessment. All of these relate to the central question of the effect of this form of assessment on student learning (both in terms of what they learn and how: of content and skills), which in the view of the tutors is far-reaching. The change has meant that the group discussions have become a more explicit and more structured part of the course than previously. As the following points suggest, in general it has been perceived as successful in terms of the quality of learning and motivation. I have added student and tutor statements to amplify each of the three points:

It encourages deep learning. Having to prepare a seminar makes us think as thoroughly about the material as if we were doing an essay on it in order to think of questions, important issues, how to structure a learning session.

It encourages commitment and mobilizes student input. Student attendance is improved, partly because of the assessment element and partly because of solidarity – 'to support colleagues', 'we didn't want to let each other down'.

There is more variety of activities – because the range of inputs is not just dependent on one person, the tutor. (Students sometimes energize the teacher!) For example, in a discussion on *Body Double* the men were asked to role-play female characters in the film and explain their experiences and the women were in the same way asked to role play the male characters.

It teaches interpersonal skills. Communication and group process skills are developed. We learned to respect each other's views. For example, one group quarrelled bitterly because they disagreed on what they should be doing but 'it was only because we cared so passionately about it'. However, 'on the day it came together because we had to do it. It went well and since then we have been best friends'.

DISCUSSION IS IMPORTANT FOR LEARNING

The principles behind the decision to change the assessment method are that we should assess what is important and that group discussion is as important a means of learning film studies as is writing.

Small peer group discussion has become commonplace in our armoury of teaching methods, not least as a response to higher numbers. *The Anatomy of Judgement* (Abercrombie, 1989), a seminal book on 'free' group discussion in higher education, first published in 1960, establishes a pedagogic rationale. Abercrombie explores the discussions of a group of medical students on a course which attempted to bring about change in the way they interpreted the world, both perceptually and conceptually.

Drawing from studies of perception, Abercrombie argues that the individual perceives the world according to pre-existing 'schemata' or basic assumptions, which 'can be regarded as tools which help us to see, evaluate and respond' (p. 28). We ignore what does not fit in with our assumptions, and learning can only proceed when there is a congruity between these and what is presented to us (this has become a familiar theme of cognitive psychology). She therefore posits two different purposes of teaching, one derived from a traditional transmission model, the other from a psychotherapy set-up. Traditionally 'the teacher's main job is to present new information in a suitably organised form and he is not much preoccupied with investigations as to how the new information comes into relationship with the old schemata' (p. 61). The free group discussion, by contrast, can enable students to begin to recognize, confront and modify their existing schemata and assumptions: 'there is no check for [one's] schemata other than talking about them, and thus comparing and contrasting them with other people's' (p. 60). This is never an easy process, and there is a tendency for the learner to resist it, but it is essential for real learning-as-change to take place. In a group discussion,

> learning depends on the fact that each student extracts something different from given information ... during discussions each student witnesses the making of several other interpretations in addition to his own and these pieces of information are added to his own store. The realisation of how these selections came to be made and the understanding of the new information, that is, linking it appropriately with his own relevant schemata, is a process of digestion (p. 73).

The process radically affects the relationship between teacher and students, who themselves increasingly take on the role of helping each other to 'digest' new information. Students take on different tasks:

> summarise discussion; bring the group back to the point; follow red herrings ... any one student may be at one moment the teacher or the pupil, and the tact, patience and skill which students severally or jointly may command when they undertake to teach another are worth seeing (p. 74).

For the tutors on the film studies programme, one of the energizing factors about the added student responsibility is that everyone (including the lecturer) becomes a learner.

This 'free group discussion' was a challenge that some students welcomed but others found very difficult. On the film studies programme it commonly provokes hostility from a few. Abercrombie suggests that the reason for students' resistance lies in a deep-seated, emotional reluctance to changing their entrenched and largely unconscious schemata. A similar argument is developed by Gibbs (1981), using George Kelly's personal construct theory, addressing the difficulty students have in changing their learning habits. In this perspective, the ways in which we view the world come to be experienced as a part of ourselves. Abercrombie's argument offers an explanation for the hostility that students can express towards small group work, which indicates the importance of its being carefully structured and introduced, especially where it is student-run. The lack of 'direction' is a commonly voiced grievance, which Abercrombie ascribes largely to student insecurity.

STUDENT STATEMENTS

Student reactions to the group work are gathered from their written individual and group statements. Below are three examples which illustrate the wide range of responses to the same exercise.

Student 1

I was most pleasantly surprised by the easy-going yet rigorously enquiring atmosphere which pervaded the running of the unit. To answer 'what have I learned from this unit through seminar experience?', I would encapsulate my answer by the following points:

1. That the method of student-led seminars breaks down the barrier between the student and the imagined opposition of the 'trans-cendental', omniscient entity (ie, the 'Teacher' so called) and thus empowers the students to take an active responsibility for their own education. Rather than the students presenting themselves to the university as an empty vessel passively awaiting to be filled by some humanistic notion of 'higher knowledge' – known only to the initiated – open group discussion based on student-researched material creates a 'democratic' area free from the imagined – or otherwise – academic, hierarchical power structures that student passivity so blindly reinforces.

2. The above is further encouraged as the students, in their role of joint-seminar leader, are placed in a position of empathy with the tutor proper. In this sense the students come to understand the perfor-mance demands placed upon the tutor and whilst this de-mystifies the imagined omnipotence of the tutor and empowers the student, it also, at the same time, encourages an affinity based not on subjection to a paternalistic 'ideological state apparatus' ie, the tutor, but on a sympathetic respect for the acquired skills of the other.

Student 2

Thinking about my individual course statement, I began to feel that it would be quite difficult to try to isolate it from the group statement; or class statement had there been one. It is almost as if I, although working on my own for most of the 'real' time, was still part of a larger whole; that my contribution based on individual research and experience became 'entwined' with others.

It occurred to me that this was no coincidence. The whole idea of film production is that a number of individuals work in smaller groups to bring about the end result; and I think this also applied to us. The teachers/ tutors (and 'co-students') wrote their lecture papers well in advance, as writers and scriptwriters do. We, the students, like actors, are put through our paces by the help of our tutors (directors) and fellow students (fellow actors) and begin to deliver a continuously more polished and thought out work as a result as we familiarize ourselves with the whole concept.

For me, film study was new and brought with it not only a new subject but also a new approach: individuals working together for the same aim – to acquire knowledge and understanding through the experience. I welcomed the opportunity with open arms and found it exciting, illuminating and rewarding.

Student 2's group

The seminar group was formed by the random method of happening to sit together.... Immediately after the first seminar we met up briefly to set the plan for the 'task' ahead. As some had read the novel, some had seen the film, some had done both, preliminary discussion took place as to the themes running through the film and the novel, and it was decided that two weeks would allow enough time ... to familiarize ourselves with both *Orlandos.*

The second meeting revealed a wealth of viewpoints which reflected our individual knowledge and life experience. After a long discussion about the points to be raised, we agreed to meet after a period of two weeks, each preparing a theme through further research for discussion. During the third, two and a bit hour conversation, in which everyone took part, we exchanged our oral and written information based on our individual research, and it became a more developed learning experience for all of us. We talked and debated (rather than explained and argued, although obviously there was some good heated element of that as well) and successfully clarified our viewpoints as to the questions we wanted to raise during the seminar.

By pooling our knowledge and supporting each other, our commitment to learning as individuals grew and was strengthened by becoming a group.

Student 3

I got quite a lot from lectures and background reading but not a great deal from seminars. As far as I can make out, possibly due to a heavy workload, the majority of students I spoke to jotted down the first idea that they had, and either quick-typed them or just wrote them down on blackboards. The basic student tactic was to avoid being seen by lecturers to be talking about anything but the subject in hand and in their own seminar [that they were responsible for organizing], kill as much time as possible with 'discussion' time before taking control (?) of the last section of the seminar. Any discussions there were polarized between several of the more talkative (dominant?) students, every seminar.

DISCUSSION

These student statements could be analysed from different perspectives: in particular, for example, they call for more knowledge about what actually went on in those seminars that could have produced such different perceptions. The student statements also, of course, raise questions about the organization of the seminars which the tutor (myself) needs to address, in particular about the organization and setting up of the work and about her own role. However, what I will concentrate on in the following remarks is what the statements themselves reveal about the small group learning.

Students 1 and 2 already have a notion of their own responsibility for both their learning and for the progress of the course. By contrast, for student 3 seminars are perceived as something that need not be taken too seriously; questions can be quickly prepared and the task then handed over to the other students on the 'day'. From an instrumental point of view this perception might be seen as reflecting the 10 per cent allocated to this part of the unit.

The attitudes expressed about the relationship between students and teachers range from the delighted sense of a new equality in student 1 to the sense expressed by student 3 of the students as schoolchildren trying to 'deceive' the teacher, to avoid being found out as not 'getting on with' the task, which is perceived as lacking in purpose. Students 1 and 2 express a sense of ownership of the process, student 3 a sense of frustrated disconnection in the comments on 'killing time' and the polarized discussions between dominant and 'other' students.

There are a number of lessons that might be drawn from these comments: first, assigning 10 per cent of the total marks for the unit to seminar performance does not, of course, guarantee the value of the group process in terms of student learning. It is hoped that the change to 20 per cent will make some difference. On the other hand, it signals that the course team attaches a certain significance to the process (not, comparatively, very much), formalizes a structuring for the seminars, and signals that seminar performance is an intrinsic component of the unit, not an 'add on'. Students are given an extrinsic reason to attend the seminars, and indeed attendance is usually high.

On the evidence of these statements, this is not, however, enough to guarantee an improvement in learning in the way that was conceived by the tutors. Student 1's work could be read as a clear confirmation of the tutors' aspirations for group work (in fact, with a slight shift in perspective, as a parody based on a confident, even playful use of literary studies discourse), while student 2's invention of a metaphor linking her experience of the process to the course content indicates a personal integration (metaphors both bring together two items and make a new construct). Both have transformed the experience into a personal synthesis. Student 3's response, however, puts paid to any incipient tutor complacency. While she too has synthesized the experience into a clear statement, it is a statement of a generally frustrating and unproductive experience. It seems to me, however, to be honest and clear enough to suggest what needs to be done to improve the experience. It is not bland like some, whose surface accounts of 'what the students did' are impossible to plumb, and which may indeed represent attempts to avoid being 'found out'.

If learning consists of a continual re-forming of the person's own conceptual schemata, I would argue that all three statements demonstrate learning in process in that all present their own model of the seminar set-up. Moreover, all demonstrate an awareness of the group process as something separate from themselves, for which they are using a meta-language, and in this sense an awareness both of the process and of themselves in relation to it.

William Perry's study of intellectual development in Harvard students (discussed by Gibbs, 1981) argues that learners proceed through a hierarchy of different attitudes to knowledge and authority from a belief in the 'right' answer of authority, through an attitude that all knowledge is relative, to a measured commitment to one's own position. If we apply this 'grading' to these student statements, 1 and 2 seem to demonstrate in different ways an assurance of one's own position, whereas statement 3 suggests an attempt to be forging a position that moves beyond that imposed by an authority, in the determination to demonstrate that the seminars are not at all how they might appear to the 'innocent' tutor. The frustration expressed in this statement, however, is that this learning has not applied to the subject matter of the seminars. It hints at a sense of the right to an experience which is as yet unmet.

SELF- AND PEER-ASSESSMENT AS OWNERSHIP

I believe that an important factor missing from the new assessment is a shift from tutor to student assessment. This was originally proposed by the tutors but rejected by students on the Board of Studies that had to agree the change. We have changed the 'what' and 'how' of assessment but not the 'who'. David Boud's and Phil Race's chapters in this volume demonstrate the negative effects on students of being assessed; the most extreme form of teacher control over the student is the exam, where the whole process, from the questions set, the timing, to the place, are all determined by the tutor. In spite of the moves to hand over to the students in this film studies programme, the tutors remain the sole assessors of the students' participation in the seminars. This is a time-consuming process, and difficult, at least for those teaching part-time, who sometimes find it hard to even identify who the students are.

A strong reason for not moving to student assessment was that the students themselves voiced unease about becoming their own – or each others' – assessors. However, I consider that the students are in at least as good a position as I am to gauge their contribution to the group process. Of course, perhaps along with the other students, I could make a judgement on how they carry out their termly organization of the whole group and make some assessment of their written statements. Yet the colleague-like relationship between tutor and student that the seminars promote is inconsistent with the tutor, in the end, acting as judge. It is no wonder that some students adopt an instrumental and even manipulative approach.

In my view a change to some form of self- and peer-assessment would be of benefit both in saving the tutors time and, particularly, in its impact on the sense of ownership and in terms of the responsibility that the change in assessment was designed to promote. Students are now expected to take more responsibility than previously for the seminar process; they are being asked to be 'adult' in their participation, in their organization of others, and in their reflection on their work. They now need to take responsibility for assessing it. Students can hardly be expected to be open – or adult – about their attitudes to knowledge if they are not, in the end, allowed to be so about their assessment. A move to self-assessment, agreed and validated by the group, seems to me to be most in the spirit of what these seminars try to achieve.

At the SEDA conference, *Assessment for Learning in Higher Education*, that led to this volume, a workshop modelled the peer group discussion and the group (of staff development professionals) assessed its own contributions. Each participant gave him or herself a grade, then discussed, reviewed, and in some cases negotiated the grade with the group. The group based their gradings on the fairly broad criteria that they were provided with from the course documentation which, in some cases, they wished to modify or expand. Everyone agreed that self-assessment backed up by peer-assessment was appropriate to the task and congruent with the learning situation, whereas tutor-assessment, coming into the group from the outside, would have felt intrusive and rather irrelevant.

Other forms of self- or peer-assessment could be used: Gibbs *et al.* (1989), for example, suggest that the tutor give the group a grade which the group members then have to divide up individually. Mathews (1994) describes the use in a Diploma in Management Studies class of a pro-forma with criteria on which students have to record, anonymously, a grade for each member – themselves and the others. The tutor has the task of interpreting the hidden agenda behind the grades and of deciding on the final grade. This, however, seem to me to be antipathetic to the mutuality that the group process is trying to build up.

The tutors may wish to retain some assessment role; I have suggested that they might assess each group's seminar organization, either formally or informally, in order to give structured feedback to the group. This group mark would give the students an 'external' starting point for their own self- and peer-assessment. The other students too, could provide feedback. It would be important not to focus too exclusively on the one-off event since the assessment is intended to cover contributions for the whole unit.

Another valid way of providing a tutor/student mix in assessment would be for the tutors to continue to assess the student statements on the basis of what students have learned from (and contributed to) the seminars. The statements that we ask them to produce could then be directed in different ways, for instance by asking for evidence for the student's stated contribution as well as for accounts of what they have 'learned', thereby encouraging a reflexive approach to the student's subject learning and to the learning process itself.

Difficulties of implementation are resolvable if the principle is accepted of the appropriateness and validity of student assessment in a set-up which demands and tries to develop student autonomy and which, in doing so, produces a situation where the students have more information about their work than do the tutors. Students may need some training in undertaking the task but self-assessment is also a transferable skill, of which they will already have experience in their lives, even if informally.

It would be interesting to surmise the effect on the student statements reproduced above if they had been written in circumstances where students were active in their own assessment. Student 1 might have had to supplement the theoretical stance and provide some concrete evidence about what she has actually done or learned during the unit. I would assume that student 2 would have been satisfied that she had provided evidence of her contribution to the work. If student 3's statement had been geared more explicitly to explaining her contribution (or lack of it) to the process she might have reviewed what happened more clearly. My hope would be – one of the points of introducing student assessment – that she and those she worked with would have been more likely to take responsibility for the process throughout. As this experience generally has demonstrated, handing over responsibility to the learner presents difficulties but they are difficulties to do with their learning development: positive difficulties, worth working on.

Chapter 11

Learning Contracts – Related Assessment Issues

Irene Harris

INTRODUCTION

My aim in this chapter is to draw attention to a number of potential tensions in the assessment process where learning contracts are used. Such tensions are, of course, apparent to differing degrees with all assessment processes. Heron (1981) and others have highlighted the assessment process as the most political of all the processes of education and one whereby issues of power are particularly significant. In earlier chapters in this volume David Boud and Phil Race have drawn attention to some of the negative effects of assessment on learning. I am sure we can all recall our own experiences of learning and assessment and the parts played, overtly and covertly, by power, politics, fear, teacher 'cues' and peer group pressure. These and other factors can turn the assessment process into a 'game', with largely unwritten rules, played by the different stakeholders in the process.

The principles behind the use of learning contracts seek to address more overtly some aspects of the 'hidden' agenda of power and politics and also to shift the balance of control of learning towards the learner. However, when learning contracts are used the negative impact of assessment does not automatically go away. It is still important to address the assessment issues and tensions if the potential learning benefits of using learning contracts are to be realized. This consideration of assessment practice needs to take account of the varied requirements of the stakeholders in the learning and assessment process – namely, learners, lecturers and the educational 'system'.

In this chapter I will firstly review the nature of learning contracts and their use in higher education, then go on to discuss their use on three particular courses, and finally draw together what I see as the main assessment-related issues which need to be considered.

147

LEARNING CONTRACTS IN HIGHER EDUCATION

An approach to self-directed learning

It is against the background of calls for more self-directed learning and for greater student responsibility, control and accountability that the use of learning contracts as a mechanism for self-directed learning can be seen to have grown. A review of the literature reveals a number of different terms used to describe such arrangements, including learning contracts or contract learning (Knowles, 1986), learning agreements (Long, 1990), or negotiable learning agreements (Race, 1992). All these terms and others are in current use and I'm sure that more 'variations on a theme' will emerge in the future.

Knowles indicates that using learning contracts is, 'an alternative way of structuring a learning experience', (1986, p. 39). He describes a typical learning contract as a mechanism which involves students in identifying and recording;

- their negotiated learning goals and objectives

- the methods by which these goals will be met

- the timescale for completion

- the evidence which will be presented to show that objectives have been achieved

- the means by which the achievement of the goals can be assessed and at what level.

The aspects of learning emphasized here, namely, content; roles and responsibilities; learning resources; and evaluation and assessment, are ones which receive attention in the wider debate about self-directed learning and the balance between teacher and learner control. Key features of learning contracts are that these issues ought to be overtly addressed and that the agreement to the contract of the various parties in the learning relationship should be written down. Supporters of learning contracts emphasize the need for parties to the contract to have a clear and shared understanding of their roles and responsibilities. As in any negotiation or agreement, the idea of a shared understanding is often easier to aim for than it is to achieve in practice. It is important to emphasize here that evaluation and assessment feature in the list of areas to be agreed upon and included in the contract. This concept of affording learners a greater say in decisions about evaluation and assessment represents a significant change to the more usual role and responsibilities of learners on qualification courses.

At its simplest, then, a learning contract can be seen as a written record of agreements negotiated between staff and students regarding the students' learning aims and objectives, the ways in which they will go about this learning and the ways in which they will evaluate these achievements. The period of time covered by a contract varies, as does the nature of the learning undertaken. Where a contract is used as part of a formal course of study, then it is argued that the lecturer needs to be satisfied that all the requirements of the course, institution and awarding body are met before agreeing to the contract (Knowles, 1986; Stephenson and Laycock, 1993).

Using learning contracts can be seen as one way of organizing learning on a more individual basis for learners within a qualification course. I found Rogers' (1983) description useful in highlighting the place of learning contracts within the educational 'system':

Contracts allow students to set goals and to plan what they wish to do. Contracts provide a sort of transitional experience between complete freedom to learn whatever is of interest and learning that is relatively free, but that is within the limits of some institutional demand or course requirement (p. 140).

This indicates to me one reason why learning contracts appear to be growing in use and gaining the support of individual lecturers, education managers and others who influence the shape of education, They can be seen as a mechanism which 'bridges' the ideals of self-directed learning and the demands of the 'system' for a rigorous approach to recording learning intentions and outcomes. The actual implementation of learning contracts and the reality of institutional and course requirements will obviously vary.

Learning contracts – a review of differences in use

Learning contracts are now used on many different courses in higher education and examples are presented and discussed by various writers, including, Baume and Brown (1992), Boud (1988a, b), Brown and Baume (1992), Hustler *et al.* (1993), Knowles (1986), Stephenson and Laycock (1993) and Tomkins and McGraw (1988). They are often used to replace more traditional, didactic approaches and they are also used to manage a variety of other learning situations on research degrees, work placements and projects.

These reviews indicate that learning contracts are used in different ways and that, as might be expected, there is considerable variation in the degree of learner control and involvement in the key areas of learning objectives, learning methods and evaluation and assessment. Five important differences are discussed below.

First, the degree of choice for students in terms of the objectives of study varies. For example, the learning objectives may be prescribed, in which case the learner's choice is limited to the learning strategy. In other cases the learner can choose from a number of pre-set objectives. Moreover, students will experience varying degrees of choice of subject matter, which will range from almost total freedom of choice to very clearly defined and pre-structured choices.

Second, there is a variety of learning outcomes that may be expected. For example, the emphasis may be on self-directed skills as an outcome or on a 'body of knowledge' or both to varying degrees. The extent to which learners can influence the type of output required will also vary. For example, on some courses they can decide the form of the learning 'output', provided it is agreed in the contract. On other courses the 'output' required for the qualification will be laid down, as an essay, dissertation, portfolio, etc.

Third, the degree to which students are involved in their own academic grading and assessment on a qualification course is very variable. Just as with any other approach to learning and assessment, there are different techniques employed and laid down in course regulation. So, on some courses the student specifies, as a part of the contracting process, the academic grade that they hope to achieve; on other courses the academic assessment is conducted by the lecturer; on some courses the final grade is open to some negotiation; and on other courses a combination of self-, peer- and tutor-assessment is used. Tomkins makes a distinction between evaluation and the academic grading, noting that, 'In contracting, the emphasis in evaluation must remain student-centred.... Grading, however, remains a complicated and thorny issue and it is at this point in the process that teacher control is most protected' (Tomkins and McGraw, 1988, p. 181).

The distinction made here between evaluation and grading, is, I feel, an important one. In practice students are often expected to evaluate their own learning but are not involved in the academic grading. However the line between evaluation and grading may well be perceived and interpreted differently by teachers and students and this can clearly influence behaviour and expectations. In this area of contracting it is most important that there is clear understanding and agreement.

Fourth, different members of staff using learning contracts on the same course will have their own ways of working with the contract. This will in turn affect the learning experience of the students.

Fifth, the style and complexity of the learning contract itself (that is to say of the document rather than the process it represents) also vary considerably from course to course. Some are very formal and a strict procedure is laid down by which they are negotiated and agreed, others are much more informal.

LEARNING CONTRACTS – SOME EXAMPLES OF CURRENT PRACTICE

Review of the use of learning contracts on three courses

As part of a wider project I examined the use of learning contracts on two undergraduate courses and one postgraduate course in my own faculty. As might be expected I found differences in practice, particularly in relation to issues of control, student choice, staff and student roles and methods of assessment. Four key points arising from my investigation are discussed below.

First, these courses are all using learning contracts in units focused on the development of employment-related skills, and there is an emphasis on skills and competence in the guidance notes to students. All of these units are compulsory elements of the courses. The need for such skills is not negotiable and the learning contract is the method by which the associated learning is managed. So, at this level there is no choice for students and the control is firmly with the staff.

Second, the courses have similar stated aims about the areas of skills to be developed. In practice students are offered different choices about which skills to develop. For example:

- On one degree course students are required to include 13 skills, which are laid down, in their learning contract, and they can choose to include more.

- On the other degree course students are given many examples of employment-related skills but there is no set list to choose from. The students have to identify two course-related skills to include in their contract.

- On the postgraduate course students chose four skills from a 'menu' of 18.

In each case the course design clearly sets limits on the choices for students.

Third, all the courses emphasize the value of learning from reflection and this value is translated into assessment requirements. Different techniques are employed to encourage reflection, including diaries and workbooks. Academic assessment includes a written reflective document on all courses. This calls to mind a number of issues, including:

- the different standards of student skills in reflection
- the difficulty of recording reflection
- the differences of value, interpretation and judgement – by staff and students
- the possible unintended imposition of staff values on students
- the temptation for students to write what they think staff expect
- the stated emphasis is on the process of reflection but assessment is of product.

Fourth, the approaches to assessment showed some similarities in that students were required to evaluate their performance, against the contract, and to present a variety of evidence to support their cases. In each case a written, reflective document was required and there were guidelines about what this should cover. In addition, students were required to submit other evidence of their learning, were given examples of the types of evidence required and were encouraged to use a variety of examples. Within the degree courses students were also assessed by an oral presentation.

On each course the academic assessment and grading was by tutors and guidelines were given about the levels of work expected for different grades. On all courses the design and operation of the assessment structure was very much controlled by the staff.

Assessment practice – points arising for consideration

In discussions with my colleagues about the assessment strategies in use on these courses a number of interesting questions emerged for further exploration, including the following.

To what degree are students actually restricted by the assessment guidelines, teacher 'cues' and examples of contracts and learning objectives in working out their own learning needs and standards? Students unused to independent learning tend to seek reassurance in the form of firmer guidelines since this represents a safer option for them. Striking a balance between clear guidelines and over-prescription is not easy.

Students using learning contracts may not have the skills required to take advantage of the choice and control available to them. In using learning contracts the aim of staff might be for students to be more self-directing, but this will not automatically happen if students are unused to independence.

Staff indicated concerns about the different approaches to assessment which could be adopted by members of a course team, and to the contracting process more generally. In essence these concerns centred upon the equity of different tutors taking different stances on academic assessment and upon differences in style with regard to teaching and guidance. This indicates that the way the various units are managed and the degree of student choice and control will be influenced by the individual members of staff as well as by the course design.

For each of these courses the use of learning contracts was intended to lead to greater involvement of students in decisions about their own learning, including evaluating their own progress against agreed learning objectives. In each case initial feedback from staff and students is very favourable. As with all courses, these are subject to on-going review and evaluation by staff and students which will lead to improvements in design and delivery – including, I'm sure, the assessment process.

It is interesting to note that the actual academic grading is in each case carried out by staff. This does not surprise me as this is often the case with examples of learning contracts written up more widely in related literature. The recurring question this raises in my mind is, how much do the perceived expectations of grading and assessment, actually alter – or indeed restrict – the nature of learning undertaken by students? I suspect that this impact is, in practice, greater than staff intended. This is a familiar concern with other approaches to learning and assessment and the same potential problems apply with learning contracts. In these circumstances, how real is the notion of increased 'learner control'?

ASSESSMENT ISSUES IN USING LEARNING CONTRACTS

What I want to do now is to pull together a summary of what seem to me to be important issues about the use of learning contracts in higher education, particularly those issues relating to assessment.

A principal idea behind the learning contract concept is that decisions about the content, method and the evaluation and assessment of learning are reached by negotiation and written down. As I have already indicated, these are important decisions in any learning situation. The contracting process should facilitate negotiation about such decisions and involve learners in this process. However, while this process may address some of the issues more overtly, it will not automatically resolve tensions and differences of view. As with other learning methods the reality for each individual using a learning contract will be different in that,

● the degree of control exercised by teachers and learners will vary

● the interpretation of roles and responsibilities will vary

● the priority given to different aims and objectives will vary.

This highlights what is for me a key issue about using learning contracts. They may give the appearance of increased learner control and self-direction and this is often one of the stated reasons for using them. However, just as with any other learning situation, the actual situation for individual learners may be very different to the outward appearance. In my view this need to look beneath the surface is heightened with learning contracts because they are so often presented as a means of self-directed learning with increased learner control that the product behind the 'label' or 'brand name' is assumed to have certain properties, when in point of fact these properties should not be taken for granted. And the approach adopted for formal assessment clearly influences the learning and the locus of control, thereby restricting the power that learning contracts have for empowering the learner.

A teacher may introduce learning contracts but then use them in a highly prescriptive way, in terms of controlling the objectives, any negotiation and the assessment process. In these circumstances the opportunities for students to be self-directing will naturally be limited. This issue is neatly encapsulated by Tomkins, in the phrase, 'letting go is sometimes the greatest challenge for the teacher' (Tomkins and McGraw, 1988, p. 177). I can relate this to my own experience and that of my colleagues when using learning contracts and other approaches to self-directed learning. In the area of assessment, 'letting go' is against the main traditions of educational practice and one which meets considerable conscious and subconscious resistance.

Learning contracts bring to the surface the ongoing debate about process and product and the emphasis on assessment that characterizes qualification courses. With learning contracts students are made more aware of their own learning process and often include the development of learning skills as part of their objectives. However, the requirement on many qualification courses is that academic grading will be based on learning outcomes which are often expressed in more traditional knowledge terms. In my view this represents a potential area of tension for learners in that they are encouraged to value and develop their process skills and to reflect formally on them, yet these are often neither formally recognized nor rewarded by the 'system'.

Differences in tutor approach to and interpretation of assessment processes, as well as in respect of other issues are familiar phenomena in education. Such differences may well be more apparent with learning contracts where the roles and responsibilities of learners and lecturers are more openly addressed. In my view such discussion is healthy, provided it is in fact open. However, the readiness and ability of different staff and students to engage in such discussion will clearly vary. The ideal of 'shared understanding' may, in reality, be difficult to attain. Indeed in the current climate of increased pressure on staff time the opportunity for such one-to-one discussion may be scarce.

A theory/practice divide may emerge. For example, the intention may be to give learners choice and control but in practice they may have less real choice, and be subject to more stringent assessment than with other methods. This may be partly due to over-specification in order to satisfy 'the system' of the standards of learning and to allay fears that learning contracts and other innovations signify an erosion of traditional academic standards.

If learning contracts are to be used most effectively it is important to take account of the different starting points and skills of staff and students on courses. Using learning contracts implies a different approach to teaching, learning and assessment and will require teachers and learners to display different skills. The concept of learning contracts implies a collaborative relationship between staff and students. It is important that time is taken to find out what the starting points and expectations of staff and students are. The implication here is that time needs to be spent preparing staff and students for the use of the learning contracts and for the different roles and responsibilities each will have. If this aspect is not dealt with, it is likely to lead to dissatisfaction for both staff and students and to a tendency to the superficial approach characteristic of a 'compliance culture' (Boud, 1988a; Hustler *et al.*, 1993; Tomkins and McGraw, 1988).

If the shift of control towards learners which is intended to result from the use of learning contracts is to be achieved, then I feel it is important to look at different ways of involving students in academic assessment. This may well present a major challenge to lecturers and the educational 'system'. It does not take much imagination to picture the potential bureaucracy which might be developed to deal with this. None the less, if the principles of self-directed learning and 'ownership' are to be realized, then this aspect of the use of learning contracts must be carefully considered.

SUMMING UP

In my view learning contracts provide a useful mechanism for the management of learning and a means to bring about greater learner responsibility and accountability. As with other approaches to teaching and learning, it is important to pay careful attention to the assessment process when they are introduced in qualification courses. By so doing we can minimize the non-productive tensions between assessment and learning, realize the potential of this approach to learning and reduce the possibility of students needing to become 'experts' in another form of the assessment 'game'.

Chapter 12

Improving Feedback
To and From Students

Nancy Falchikov

INTRODUCTION

It is widely recognized that learning depends on feedback to the learner
and that providing quick and helpful feedback to students is extremely
beneficial. It is also acknowledged that, in an expanding educational
system, it is becoming more and more difficult to maintain levels and
quality of feedback. Students have been found to benefit from an
increased involvement in the assessment of their own work and the work
of others. However, students too often are a neglected resource in
present day higher education.

In this chapter, a study of peer feedback marking (PFM) which
required students to provide feedback to their peers is described. The
study involved third-year students and related to assessment of individual
oral presentations. Marks awarded by staff and peer markers were found
to resemble each other. Student evaluations of the scheme of PFM suggested that they perceived it to have been beneficial. They reported that
they had experienced an increase in autonomy and an increase in
learning as a consequence of participation in the scheme. There is a great
deal too that we as teachers can learn from students about the level and
quality of feedback they find most useful.

Bruner (1970, p. 120) stated that learning depends upon 'knowledge
of results, at a time when, and at a place where, the knowledge can be
used for correction'. In other words, learning depends upon feedback to
the learner. A number of factors can influence the degree to which
feedback can be more or less useful to the recipient. For example, the
location and timing of feedback are important, and also what Bruner
describes as 'the form in which the corrective information is received'
(p.121). The term 'feedback' was originally coined by Norbert Weiner in
1948, and introduced into the social sciences by Lewin (Jacobs, 1974). It
has been formally defined as signifying 'verbal and nonverbal responses

from others to a unit of behavior provided as close in time to the behavior as possible, and capable of being perceived and utilised by the individual initiating the behavior' (Benne *et al.*, 1964). In other words, feedback to students should be provided quickly and be useful and accessible to them.

Jacobs (1974) identifies two major properties of feedback: the informational and hedonic components. The former provides the data which enable recipients to modify, adapt and improve their work, and the latter acts to influence their motivation. Both aspects are important. Positive feedback can act as a general 'reinforcer' and increase the likelihood of the desirable behaviour being repeated. However, negative feedback, in the context of T-groups at least, has been found to lead to self-devaluative responses which can both interfere with the reception of information contained in the feedback and, in some cases, lead to escape, avoidance and denial on the part of the recipient (Jacobs, 1974). Jacobs and his co-workers also found that high levels of tension were associated with verbal delivery of negative feedback, and as Bruner (1970) argues, 'one state in which information is least useful is when the learner is impelled by strong drive and anxiety' (pp. 121–122).

Common sense suggests that, when feedback is mixed, it is better to receive positive elements before negative. This would seem particularly important with respect to learner confidence and self-esteem. When feedback includes both positive and negative elements, studies of the ordering of delivery of the two types have found that the order of delivery does, indeed, affect the way the feedback is received (Jacobs, 1974); increased self-esteem and a reduction in anxiety are associated with giving positive feedback first. In addition, there are other order-of-presentation effects. Cohesiveness of groups and individual perceptions of the credibility of the person delivering the feedback have also been found to be affected by the ordering of elements. Further studies by Jacobs *et al.* (reported in Jacobs, 1974) found that strong feelings of group cohesiveness developed in significantly larger numbers of members who had received positive feedback followed by negative (delivered by the same person) than in members receiving feedback in the reverse order. Moreover, in the former group, the person delivering the negative feedback second was rated as more credible by group members than the person delivering the negative feedback first was by learners exposed to that treatment.

Written delivery of feedback differs from verbal delivery in that it has the advantage of persisting through time and being more resistant to selective or faulty memory. Many teachers work hard to supply helpful comments, and assume that students read and act upon feedback given to them. However, the growing suspicion that this perfect feedback loop may not always function is supported by a review of research by Mac-Donald (1991). Study findings showed that teachers, in fact, often write confusing and contradictory comments, or superficial comments that focus on surface errors. Similarly, Turner (1993) found that written feedback to students was very variable in quality and often negative in tone. MacDonald also found that students often do not read their teachers' feedback, and when they do so, often misunderstand it. Even when the feedback comments are read and understood, they are rarely acted upon. Least surprising of MacDonald's findings is that the student's primary interest when receiving returned coursework is the grade awarded. Clearly some initiative is needed to break this unhelpful pattern of behaviour.

The language in which feedback is delivered is an important variable. Stones (1970) argues that the language of the teacher is one of the most important elements in the learner's concept formation. More than a simple 'correct' or 'incorrect' response is required. Explanations for both types of response are desirable. In Chapter 2, in this volume, in which he criticizes many assessment practices, David Boud refers to Rorty's 'final vocabulary' (Rorty, 1989), the 'set of words' employed by humans to justify their actions and beliefs and to 'formulate praise of our friends and contempt for our enemies' (p. 73). Part of one's final vocabulary is made up of terms such as 'good' and 'right', and another part of terms like 'professional standards' and 'rigorous', terms Rorty believes cannot be supported without recourse to circular argument. The language of feedback to students too often takes the form of a word or phrase from the marker's final vocabulary, usually accompanied by a grade at the end. Assessment of this type merely serves to lock an already closed door, rather than to open up possibilities of change and learning. Brown and Knight (1994) endorse the growing view that such 'skimpy comments' cannot be rated as feedback worthy of the name.

THE EDUCATIONAL CONTEXT

The educational context of Britain in the 1990s presents a major problem for teachers determined to take formative assessment seriously and provide useful and quick feedback to their students. Improving student learning, encouraging deep rather than surface learning, and nurturing critical abilities and personal transferable skills require time. However, in an expanding higher education system with increased student numbers and larger classes, the conscientious teacher is faced with a problem. Larger classes lead to more marking and, if properly done, it takes more time. What is the teacher to do? The solution of taking even more time cannot be applied indefinitely. Decreasing the amount of feedback to each student in order to complete the task in the limited time available is clearly undesirable, given the great potential of feedback in formative assessment.

STUDENT INVOLVEMENT IN ASSESSMENT

We know that the assessment demands placed on students influence the type of learning which takes place (Laurillard, 1984; Ramsden, 1986), and the MacFarlane Report (1992) on teaching and learning in higher education argues that assessment is the single most influential factor on student learning. Devolving some responsibility for assessment to students is often seen as a means of enhancing learning (Boud, 1988b; Falchikov, 1986, 1988). Student involvement in assessment can take the form of a variety of non-traditional methods such as self-assessment, peer-assessment or collaborative assessment. Thus, it may be that we can go some way towards solving the problem of providing quick and plentiful feedback to students by involving the students themselves and tapping the resources they bring to the learning environment. The overwhelming view, arrived at after observing the results of over 20 years of peer-assessment studies, is that peer-assessment is generally a useful, reliable and valid exercise in variety of contexts (eg, Falchikov, 1986; Forehand *et al.*, 1982; Gray, 1987; Korman and Stubblefield, 1971; Linn *et al.*, 1975; Mast and Bethart, 1978; Morton and Macbeth, 1977). Feedback from students indicates that they appear to perceive peer-assessment as beneficial, providing an insight into how a peer approaches and completes a task. Moreover, peer-assessment, involving as it does a number of markers, is rated as being fairer than traditional teacher marking (Falchikov, 1986; submitted for publication).

Few student evaluations of peer-assessment are reported, but those that are available suggest that students experience more benefits than they have reservations. However, feedback from students also suggests that one aspect of peer group assessment presents them with a problem. They do not enjoy the idea of 'marking down or failing a peer', particularly in the context of a small, well-established group. This feature may account for both the difficulties experienced by students in awarding a grade and a tendency towards over-marking that I've encountered. After seeing the results of earlier studies of self- and peer-assessment (eg, Falchikov, 1986), I concluded that some aspects of peer group assessment required modification, and devised the scheme of peer feedback marking (PFM).

PFM was designed to build on the strengths of peer-assessment while minimizing the problem of the reluctance of students to mark their peers. The PFM scheme retains the sharing of information aspects of peer-assessment which students appear to enjoy and benefit from, and introduces the requirement for critical feedback as well as, or instead of, the awarding of a mark. In PFM, students are required to analyse each presentation immediately it is completed, and identify a strength and a weakness. Feedback is recorded in written form so that presenters have a permanent record, and delivered orally at the time. The ordering of the elements of feedback ('strength' followed by 'weakness') is designed to build up the confidence of the receiver and increase the chances of the more useful negative feedback being registered and acted upon. Moreover, the requirement to provide feedback is designed to aid the concentration of the audience and make their learning more active.

PEER FEEDBACK MARKING OF AN INDIVIDUAL ORAL PRESENTATION

Participants

Participants in this scheme were 13 third-year students of human developmental psychology (12 female, one male) studying for a degree in biological science at Napier University, Edinburgh. Their mean age was 20 years 11 months. Students were required to carry out an individual library-based exercise, produce a written account of their work and give a 10-minute oral presentation to the rest of the class later in the term.

Preparation and implementation

Assistance was given to students to help them prepare for the task. Before the first presentation all students were asked to think about oral presentations they had given or attended in the past, and to identify the characteristics of a good presentation. A short list of relevant criteria was compiled. Next, students were reminded of the marking bands in use at Napier. Finally, copies of a peer-assessment form were circulated, which asked students to identify a strength and a weakness, and to suggest how the presentation might be improved. They were then asked to award a mark out of 20. After each student's presentation, peers completed the assessment form. Assessors were required to add their names to assessment forms, but were assured that these would be removed before feedback was passed on to presenters, in order to encourage honesty. Written assessments were also made independently by the lecturer, using the same assessment form. Oral feedback, based on the written assessments, was given immediately on completion of each presentation. All assessment sheets were collected, and mean peer marks calculated. These student-derived marks contributed 20 per cent to the grade for this piece of coursework, the remaining 80 per cent being awarded by the lecturer for the written account.

An evaluation sheet was distributed to all students at the next meeting after completion of the exercise. Peer-assessment lists of 'best features' and 'weaknesses' relating to each presentation were anonymized and returned to students along with mean peer-assessment marks.

Treatment of results

Comparisons were made between mean peer and lecturer marks. 'Best features' and 'weaknesses' listed for each presentation were grouped into a number of categories, and the degree of inter-rater agreement calculated. Comparisons were made between lecturer and student comments.

Results

Comparisons of mean peer mark and lecturer mark showed that differences between the two marks were small, varying between +2.1 (+10.5 per cent of the total marks available) and –0.6 (–3.0 per cent). In nine cases, the mean peer mark exceeded that of the lecturer ('over-marking'), though by 1 mark only (5.0 per cent). In the remaining four cases 'under-marking' occurred, and the lecturer's mark exceeded the mean peer mark by 0.6 mark (3.0 per cent). The overall difference was +0.5 of a mark (2.5 per cent). The distribution of marks over the degree classification ranges indicated no difference between the lecturer and mean peer mark.

Thus, as in other studies of peer-assessment, mean peer marks were not too dissimilar from lecturer marks. However, some suggestion of 'over-marking' persisted, but rather less than on previous occasions, in spite of the requirement in the present study to mark out of 20 rather than the wider percentage range.

Features of student feedback

Features of presentations identified and listed by students fell into a number of categories, which reflected the criteria relating to a good oral presentation they had identified earlier. Each feature had a positive and a negative pole: for example, positive comments on *Understanding and structure* included, 'Very interesting. I could relate to it', and 'Easy to follow'. Negative comments included, 'It was hard to understand the study', and 'Confused and confusing.' Other categories were *Delivery*

('Well presented. Very good overheads and handouts', 'Read straight from notes, with little eye contact'), *Amount of material included* ('Just the right amount. All the information was relevant', 'Lasted a bit too long'), *Knowledge* ('Seemed to know the study well', 'Seemed like they did not know what was coming next'), *Topic* ('Intrinsic interest in the topic', 'Good, hard hitting information'). *Effort* expended on the presentation featured very little in ratings, attracting one mention only.

The degree of agreement between peers over strengths and weaknesses of presentations varied from 25 per cent to 100 per cent. The greater the variety of features identified, the lower the percentage agreement. For more detail see Falchikov (submitted for publication).

Student evaluation of the scheme

The best-liked features of peer feedback marking generally fell into one of two groups (*Fairness* and *Feedback as an aid to learning*), in roughly equal numbers. Least-liked features of the scheme similarly fell into two categories (*Marking friends* and *Analytical skills*). Student comments from the first category were reminiscent of reactions to earlier peer-assessment schemes and included:

> Some of the marks given were a bit high. Some people perhaps felt embarrassed judging their peers.

> I find it difficult to assess people as fairly as I want to. You may feel obliged to friends – everybody knows everybody's writing.

Work groups of established friends may become less of a 'problem' in the future where very large classes become the norm, although working together in a randomly constituted group may subsequently lead to friendships. The lecturer has the choice of determining initial group composition so as to avoid friendship groups. Fear of the lack of anonymity will recede as class sizes increase and more demands are placed on students to word-process their essays or record assessments directly into a computer. However, it can be argued that learning how to make criticism in a diplomatic manner is a useful skill in itself.

A comparison of peer feedback marking and traditional marking

PFM was seen as conferring more benefits on users and to have fewer disadvantages than traditional marking. It was rated as making the user think and learn more, and become more independent, confident and critical than does the traditional scheme. Some lack of confidence was expressed by students about bias and accuracy in PFM compared with traditional marking. It is possible that this will decrease with further experience and practice of using PFM.

DISCUSSION

A comparison of lecturer and mean peer marks indicated that, overall, there was reasonable agreement between the two, but that some degree of over-marking on the part of students, previously found in peer-assessment studies, persisted. Student feedback was also seen to resemble lecturer feedback in many respects. Students felt that PFM conferred more benefits (and fewer disadvantages) than traditional marking. They believed that they thought more and learned more when engaging in PFM than when traditional marking is carried out. Similarly, students rated themselves as having increased their independence and critical abilities by participating in the scheme.

To what extent does PFM overcome the problems encountered in earlier studies of peer-assessment? The main problem of peer-assessment – the reluctance of students to award marks – does not go away in PFM (unless, of course, the requirement for awarding marks is removed). However, it seems that the task of marking is made a little less difficult by the discussion of criteria and critical analysis which precede it. In this study, the peer-derived proportion of the coursework mark was small, which may have contributed to the students' ability to resist any tendency to over-mark. The similarity of student and lecturer marks in the present study of PFM may also, in part, be due to the preliminary work of ensuring that students were familiar with the meanings we attach to coursework and exam marks. However, the use of a final-year honours degree classification of marks with first-year students brings with it its own problems. It may well be unwise to 'label' students early in their careers, particularly at a time before they have had a chance to assess their performance levels for themselves. We must not forget the power of self-fulfilling prophesy.

The tasks which make up the scheme of PFM appeared to have served the purpose for which they were designed. For example, the requirement of peer assessors to provide immediate written feedback to presenters has a number of advantages. First of all, the presentation was fresh in the mind of assessors. Second, audience concentration seemed to be sharpened. Reflection and critical analysis were essential in order to complete the assessment task, and as assessment sheets carried the name of the assessor, it is possible that they felt the need to write something in order to avoid the embarrassment of handing in a blank sheet. Finally, the task of giving oral feedback was made easier by students having completed the written task first. The fear of having nothing to say, or of 'drying up' due to nervousness was removed.

Hedonic benefits associated with delivering positive feedback first were evident in this study. All student presenters seemed pleased to hear a public statement of the strengths of their work, and none seemed overwhelmed by the negative aspects identified. Reducing anxiety is particularly important in the context of oral presentations, given reports of the stress associated with this activity that is experienced by students. The question as to whether presenters subsequently acted upon the advice given to them, of course, remains open.

In terms of the language in which feedback was expressed, it appeared that students had learned to use 'lecturese'. As we have seen, student and lecturer feedback was often very similar, and it was often difficult to separate the two types. Very few examples of one-word 'final vocabulary' judgements were found. Students supplied more positive feedback than negative, suggesting that they found it easier to be complimentary than critical. It was also noted that, when making critical comments, some students expressed themselves in tentative ways, often 'excusing' the peer for the behaviour criticized. Examples of this tendency included:

The presenter did not look at the audience *much*, but *tended* to read from notes. *She was probably very nervous.*

It was *a bit* confusing. Or *maybe I was confused.* It's difficult to keep up the concentration. (Emphases added.)

Results of the content analysis of feedback statements suggested that there may be an 'hierarchy of feedback'. Feedback which focused on presentation and delivery tended to feature prominently in student feedback, suggesting that these issues need to be addressed before attention can be paid to others. It sometimes appeared that only when delivery was good or adequate did students look beyond it to issues of structure and content.

Given that change is at the heart of learning, it seems very likely that recommendations about strategies for improvement are the most useful of all types of feedback. However, positive feedback seems to be more readily supplied than are suggestions for improvement. Some modifications to the PFM system are required to address this issue. A simple change to the peer feedback assessment form may go some way towards achieving the aim of improving the quality and usefulness of feedback. The removal of the term 'weakness' and increased emphasis on the question, 'How might the presentation be improved?' may encourage all providers of feedback to meet the need for suggestions to help individuals achieve this end. Similarly, more emphasis on this issue during preparatory sessions, where students could be asked about what sort of feedback they find useful, and staff being given the opportunity to explain what it is they are trying to achieve, may help work towards the same goal. However, previous research on teacher provision of, and student reactions to, feedback (eg, MacDonald, 1991) suggests that simple measures may not be enough. Further work on the match and mismatch between student feedback needs and supply is recommended.

However, PFM seems to be a useful addition to the range of assessment options available to lecturers. An important strength of the scheme seems to be related to the enhancement of student learning by means of reflection, analysis and diplomatic criticism.

NOTES

1   Many ideas and issues raised in my SEDA conference workshop have influenced the writing of this chapter. Thanks are due to all workshop participants. Thanks, also, to Greg Michaelson for helpful comments on an earlier draft.

2   A more detailed description and discussion of my first study of PFM is to be found in Falchikov (submitted for publication).

3   Thanks are due to David Boud for introducing me to the ideas of Richard Rorty, which reminded me of the reasons why I chose to become a psychologist rather than a philosopher.

Chapter 13

The NCVQ Model of Assessment at Higher Levels

Romla Hadrill

INTRODUCTION

A consensus seems to be emerging regarding the concept and delivery of quality in education. In simple terms the view might be expressed as:

- education is about learning

- within the process of learning, assessment occupies a central role

- much current assessment practice is not conducive to optimizing learning

The implications of such a view are that there is a need for change in both assessment practice and in the preparation of persons involved in it. Issues surround the definition of good practice in the methodology of assessment and in human resource development. These are not simply technical issues but require thought about the values attaching to learning and its assessment.

Earlier chapters have addressed the relationship between assessment and learning and provide examples of assessment methods which better facilitate learning. What is offered in this chapter is compatible with and supportive of those values and practices, while seeking to professionalize assessment and enhance assessor professionalism. This chapter seeks to define ways in which the consensus can be operated and explores the mechanisms of strategic control and delivery of assessment reforms within the framework of an outcomes approach and the articulation of those outcomes as competences.

The National Council for Vocational Qualifications (NCVQ) has led the field in this area through its work on National Vocational Qualifications (NVQs) and, more recently on General National Vocational Qualifications (GNVQs). The suitability of the NCVQ model of assessment of learning and the development of a national standards framework is considered and supported with reference to current practice and emerging developments.

WHAT IS OUTCOMES-BASED EDUCATION (OBE)?

'Outcomes-based education' has been used to refer to a range of conceptions and activities related to education and training. Properly applied the term refers to a process in which the criteria for assessment are written in the form of learning outcomes. Learning outcomes, therefore, are statements describing what the learner knows, understands or can do. Examples might be, 'has expressed aims and objectives clearly and appropriately'; 'has understood and demonstrated integrity'.

Once the learning has been acquired, demonstrated and verified it can be accredited and formally acknowledged. Necessary features of assessment within this approach consist of clarity of definition of the desired outcomes and a capacity for measuring or for providing evidence of their attainment. Assessor and assessed are mutually accountable for actions taken in relation to these 'visible' criteria.

Input or outcomes?

In curricular terms a distinction can be made between OBE statements of achievement models and the more traditional model employing aims and objectives or, as these may be seen, statements of teaching intent. Lack of precision and detailed definition in their function as planning objectives is likely to make such aims and objectives largely uncheckable. It is normally not expected that diagnostic assessment will be carried out to see whether they have become *learned* outcomes and there is no formal recognition of their acquisition – or absence!

Even brief analysis of the traditional model indicates that the locus of control lies firmly with the teacher whose generation of learner-dependency arises from her/his determination of pace, sequence and content of teaching input. The implicit assumption is, at best, that learning proceeds in a linear fashion from stage to stage and that all learners follow the same route at the same pace. A pause for consideration quickly suggests this is not the case!

The potential of OBE, indeed that which identifies it as 'good practice', is that it facilitates the relocation of control and shares power between the learner and advocate. Alignment of flexible learning and assessment strategies with the attainment of pre-specified outcomes requires careful planning, support and management. In recognizing differing learner needs in style, pace and detail and in making available alternatives and support structures, a closer form of management becomes a prerequisite and carefully negotiated stages of review and intervention become a necessity.

While these two models of assessment arise from differing conceptions of the teaching and learning relationship and of the roles of respective participants in that process, most of us, as practitioners, would locate ourselves somewhere along the continuum. We are neither complete traditionalists nor willing converts to outcomes, particularly when outcomes imply or involve competences.

Assessment of outcomes

Outcomes clarify and identify the learning acquired during a process of education or training. Acquiring a mastery of these outcomes is seen as the goal of this process. Their acquisition may be dependent upon or independent of teaching and the intentions of teachers.

Assessment of learners against learning outcomes can be used to measure:

- the efficiency of input against output (both teacher and learner input)

- the extent of mastery of required learning

- the degree and precise definition of non-mastery.

Given clear articulation of outcome requisites, assessment may be used for summative purposes or have a diagnostic and formative function. While outcomes may guide assessment for any of these purposes, it is widely thought that it is not appropriate for any one assessment task to try and carry more than one of these purposes at a time. A task that is intended to have, say, formative and summative functions tends to work out as a compromised formative or as a compromised summative task. When the purpose is formative, the *process* of assessment is a major mechanism through which reflectivity can be developed and evidenced. Correctly formulated, the outcomes approach constitutes a precise form of criterion-referencing, combining the underlying value-orientation of efficient and effective practice with clear and standardized meanings. Demanding in its requirements that learning be valid when judged against the explicit criteria embodied in OBE, it implies high levels of accountability by all parties for their decision making about learning and assessment. By way of comparison with the norm-referenced basis of much traditional assessment, which does little to empower learners, a criterion- or outcomes-based model is accessible to learners, may empower them and offers a more egalitarian approach to the relationship between power and the process of assessment.

From quality control and equality of opportunity perspectives, the outcomes model of assessment seems to have clear potential for 'good practice'.

NCVQ – MODEL AND VALUES

It should be noted that, although support is here being expressed for the *model* of assessment within the NCVQ structure, important questions remain.

- What determines appropriateness and legitimacy of *content* of learning and assessment?

- What should be the framework in which the model is implemented and its content articulated?

These are, most obviously, questions about structure, pedagogy and ideology.

The NCVQ model of competence-based education and training (CBET) is an intricately systemized structure centred around criterion-referenced assessment. This statement, as a brute fact, gives it a hallmark of quality. In the current educational climate this marks it out as an achievement-oriented approach to learning and assessment. However, there is a danger of an accompanying distraction and disengagement from vital questions about the ideological and value-orientation of NVQs.

The direct translation of market forces into funding and achievement-based models of resourcing has already moved large sectors of post-compulsory education and training into an outcomes approach to learning and assessment which is sharply competence-focused. Refinement and consolidation are evident on both a horizontal axis extending vocationalism into new occupational and professional dimensions and vertically in terms of extending access to OBE and in terms of its reach upwards to levels 4 and 5, that is into the areas already colonized by higher education. Measurement through outcomes has become politically imperative and is evidenced in such initiatives and developments as:

- The National Curriculum for schools is centred upon the measurement of achievement through attainment targets which can, in some cases, be mapped directly on to elements of competence described within GNVQ core skills.

- GNVQs are available at foundation level for 14+ and at intermediate and advanced levels, paralleling academic qualifications at GCSE and 'A' levels.

- National Education and Training Targets, which are revolutionizing work-based learning and assessment.

Within higher education, benchmarks of quality are increasingly being defined in terms of outcomes as output indicators of performance.

While ideological concerns drive NVQ developments, we might bear in mind that there are no value-free educational expressions and therefore consider some suspension of scepticism about OBE. Conceptually, there is no necessary connection between model and mission, though in practice one *is* contextualized by the other. However, I suggest that the question centres around scrutiny of the NCVQ model as a mechanism detached from its implementation – could it work for us? A model, like a building, might be acclaimed for design and architectural features independent of what it houses. There seems little doubt that the NCVQ model offers the most rigorous and coherent interpretation of criterion-referenced assessment currently in use in the UK.

Design characteristics

Before detailed consideration of the NCVQ architecture, some basic design features are worth noting for comparison with notions of 'good practice' that have been emerging within this book and elsewhere. NCVQ is concerned to promote:

- input-output efficiency and effectiveness

- maximal access to learning and assessment

- credit accumulation and transfer

- the separation of learning from teaching

- the validation and accreditation of relevant prior learning

- removal of barriers to access

- meticulous quality control in assessment and accountability.

Though this is not an exhaustive inventory inclusive of NCVQ principles, nor is it exclusive, since some of these principles are shared by other projects. However, developments continue and the distinctiveness of NVQs grows as the model becomes more elaborated and more sophisticated.

NVQ architecture

Within the outcomes approach evolved by the NCVQ, outcomes are descriptors of essential work functions and are referred to as 'competences'. Through NVQ usage the term 'competence' has assumed a vocational definition. As Jessup (1991) points out 'Being competent means performing to professional or occupational standards'. From a process of 'functional analysis' of occupations, work roles and functions are analysed and disaggregated into statements of competent performance within a specified occupational area. Used as a process for the analysis and definition of the work function of, say, the 'staff developer', the method can describe operational parameters and both articulate and communicate conceptions of practice. In order to do this functional analysis, use is made of trigger questions to develop an inventory of outcomes against which comparisons and audits can be matched:

- What is the key purpose of this work?

- What are its primary functions (expressed as roles)?

- What are their subdivisions (tasks/responsibilities)?

- What are the contexts or settings in which these are performed (statements of range, for example, locations, types of people, knowledge, performance)?

Figure 13.1 indicates the relationship between the process of deconstruction of work functions and the structure of the model.

Units of competence defining major work roles contain clusters of elements of competence, each describing a task essential to the work role. In turn, they are supported by performance criteria. Each performance criterion defines the standard of performance required by the element of competence. This is then further detailed by the range statement which explains the range of applications of the element and primary contextual variations within which the competent performer might be able to work.

Job description	*Title/model/key – purpose statement*
Major work roles	Units of competence
Tasks related to each work role	Elements of competence
Task specifications	Performance criteria/range statement

Figure 13.1   *The structure of the NVQ model of functional analysis*

Ideological implications

Capable of delivering good practice in assessment in a *procedural* sense, the product-knowledge base of the NCVQ has always been contentious within educational circles. *How* to assess has appeared to be a less difficult concern than *what* to assess, although this has also proved contentious. Of course, questions of how and what are not as readily separated as this might seem to imply. Competence, evidence and range require particularization and it is here in 'the drift towards a narrow utilitarian curriculum in all sectors of the post-compulsory [education] system' (Ecclestone, 1994) that CBET has received most criticism. Questions about what should be assessed and learned arise from views about what it is appropriate to know. The contextualization, therefore, of any process of assessment is always dependent on notions of received knowledge as voiced and disseminated by those empowered to make and implement decisions. In this way, as knowledge-and-control theorists have long maintained, 'knowledge' exists as a reflection of power relations in society. It is relative, never absolute. The NCVQ contextualization of its own model, firmly rooted in vocationalism, constitutes one particular interpretation of knowledge and is as relative as any other value system. Its tenets are shared, endorsed and promoted by powerful agencies in society though they have not, in the main, included academia. The NCVQ's rationale relies upon the ethic of vocational utilitarianism, of which it has been seen as an advocate: its selection and formulation of knowledge, articulated in statements of competence, celebrates and circumscribes vocational priorities at the levels of worker, employer and state. These priorities are premised on the belief that 'knowledge' should, most importantly, be of extrinsic worth and, wherever possible, should be occupationally transferable. This has presented an irrevocable challenge to the old educational settlements serving the demands of a liberal ideology and has thereby disturbed traditional values.

Initially, the analyses of work functions for lower levels of occupations, that is non-professional levels (NVQ levels, 1, 2 and 3), were performance-focused and produced statements of competence that were quickly criticized as narrow, mechanistic and behavioural. The damage had been done as rejection by some professions took the form of condemning what was seen as a return to 'behavioural objectives' as curricular outcomes, with the result that vocational training activists were dismissed a perpetrators of subversive practices. It has been acknowledged – and presumably was always recognized by functional analysts – that appropriate behavioural performance requires and presupposes cognitive underpinning. A major divide in opinion seemed to centre around the issue of what was to count as evidence of this cognitive underpinning. Simply expressed, the point at issue was whether knowledge was taken to be implicit in performance or whether it most be explicated and evidenced separately and additionally. Early NVQ assessment strategy at levels 1–3 assumed that it was legitimate to infer that sufficient underpinning knowledge was present if there was evidence of competence through performance. This issue has been much debated and has become a major cause of dissent and disagreement between vocationalists and academics. The result is a growing agreement that cognitive foundations of performance should be made overt, should be separately evidenced and separately assessed. A further resolution of the knowledge-performance issue has taken place through the development of the vocationally broader GNVQs, which contain units of core skill competences, and through the development of standards for higher level NVQs, which have required the development of an essentially more sophisticated epistemology. So, at professional competence levels (4 and 5), with their expressed equivalence to degrees and higher degrees, considerable development work is under way. Examples of current projects include:

● NCVQ Consultation Paper on GNVQ Level 4 (Universities' Staff Development Unit of the CVCP)

● a feasibility study on the application of higher level NVQs/SVQs to training programmes for staff in higher education

● task force work on NVQs/SVQs

● Staff and Education Development Association consideration of the relationship between higher education, staff development and higher level NVQs.

THE ASSESSMENT OF COMPETENCE AND PROFESSIONALISM

Within education and training, the effectiveness of the preparation of professionals is determined by the extent to which appropriate and discernible professionalization has taken place in the would-be professional. If this statement is accepted it presupposes that effective learning for the professions involves the support of persons who understand the discharge of that professionalism. An effective professional development programme might, therefore, involve:

● the existence of a shared definition of 'professionalism'

● the means of bringing about its acquisition

● reliable means of checking professional attainment.

At base these may be seen as questions of value, input and delivery and quality control. As professionals wishing to develop professionalism in others, we are required to consider the suitability of emerging outcomes-focused approaches for the dispensation and accreditation of professionalism, in particular that of the NCVQ.

Certain conclusions might be drawn from a review of current NVQ developments. If an indicator of progress consists of the degree of support received from within the professions, it seems that NCVQ is on the up-turn. Despite some ill-informed criticism, most notably the recent Dispatches Report on Education 'All Our Futures' (Channel Four Television, 1993), there is an impressive growth and increased take-up of NVQs in the professions as part of human resource development programmes. Within the education profession there has been increased incorporation by practitioners of NVQs into their portfolios, while academics involved in research and development studies continue to refine and tailor competence constructs to reflect accurately the nature of professional practice. An important point to note here concerns the nature of the relationship between the professions and competence. Expressed simply, it is that professionalism *implies* competence. Any profession's self-image involves seeing itself, both individually and corporately, as competent; a perception shared by the public whose understanding of professional as opposed to non-professional centres upon the expectation that professionals will display competence. In general usage the terms 'professional' and 'competence' are synonymous, making it logical to elucidate professional practice through statements of competence that together describe the function of that profession.

In order to sustain confidence in its approach to the occupational mapping of professions, NCVQ needs to address the following:

- The formulation of a shared definition of 'professionalism' founded upon consensus about what constitutes professional value, which is to say that those ethics or codes of practice to which professionals adhere need to be taken into account. This might involve identifying core values that are generally endorsed and professionally transferable (see, for example, Winter, 1995). Any values identified as core would need to encapsulate and express the expectations of all stakeholders in any area of professionalism and all professions. Values identified as specific to individual professions would sit alongside these core value competences, thereby giving scope for dissent and pluralistic practice.

- The accurate formulation of knowledge, skill and capability competences of specific occupational areas within the professions in ways that make them clear and accessible.

● A robust quality control system allowing monitoring and auditing, assessment of attainment and standardization of verification and recording procedures.

Recent and current work commissioned for national standards development shows recognition of issues surrounding the development and assessment of professional competences and some impressive results (for example, Eraut, 1994a; Eraut and Cole, 1993). Acknowledging the importance of coping with the ethical dimension of occupational standards, the Employment Department has sponsored reviews of work in this area. In particular, the work undertaken by Eraut (1994a) explores the ethical foundations of the work of a profession and its expressions in national standards of competence. Eraut identifies four overlapping sets of values underpinning ethical issues in the workplace, superimposes these on the framework of general social values and discusses their incorporation into the architecture of the NVQ model. He concludes that the relationship between occupational standards incorporating ethics and extant practice within higher education in the development of codes of conduct, accountability statements and corporate missions is a complex one that is crucial to the effectiveness and credibility of occupational standards. Yet, it is both appropriate and essential that professional codes based upon ethical practice are incorporated within relevant occupational standards, for they offer an important opportunity to redress the deficiencies of the unregulated market.

QUALITY

More often than not discussion of quality in education has been taken to mean quality of teaching. This book presupposes as its underlying concern that a key issue is how best to improve the quality of learning and it may be that focusing upon the provision of 'quality' teaching does not provide an appropriate solution to this. A central assumption within these chapters is that the design and practice of assessment has a necessary relationship to the quality of learning. Thinking has moved away from traditional models of assessment and has perhaps reached its furthest point of departure within this chapter with its conception of assessment as *support for learning*. The assertion being made here is that systems that assess candidates in relation to the performance norms of other candidates, referencing against changing standards, are not only wasteful and inappropriate but lack credibility and compatibility with current expectations of quality. The mystique of (norm-referenced) assessment strategies aimed at exclusion and exclusivity needs to be replaced by (criterion-referenced) processes embracing responsibility, accountability and entitlement values if a commitment to egalitarian support for learners and learning is to be sustained.

When the outcomes of learning are clearly specified, as they are in the NCVQ model, assessment is based directly on those outcomes. Expectations and criteria of required attainment are clear and open. Outcomes-based assessment lends itself to continuous use for both formative and summative purposes and involves mastery learning in the sense that all the stated outcomes should be covered and attained rather than just a sample of them, as is typically the case with traditional assessment. Since the target learning is clear from the outset, it is not necessary to pre-define the route candidates take to reach it. There is scope for flexibility, thanks to the assumptions that learning need not be a linear progression, that not all learners learn in the same way at the same pace and that they do not always need to be synchronized through whole-group learning activities. Strategies of reviewing and analysing need, self-evaluation, action planning and contracting may be introduced and managed by the learning mentors. Through learning in this way layers of understanding, skill and knowledge might be developed as supported learner-centred activities encourage learners towards greater reflectivity and understanding.

Within the NCVQ model, assessment is viewed as the collection of evidence to support claims of the attainment of criteria of competence and natural sources within the learner's 'work' base can be drawn upon to provide such evidence. It might include performance observation, oral questioning, documentary evidence, artefacts, simulations and witness testimony. Written tests and examinations are fully acceptable examples of evidence but they are optional, being dependent on candidate choice. 'Instead of allowing the assessment to define the standards, the standards now define what needs to be assessed' (Jessup, 1991, p.49).

VALIDITY

A major distinguishing feature of the NCVQ assessment model is its emphasis on validity. Validity is judged by the extent to which an assessment instrument measures what it is intended to measure. Whereas the concept of 'reliability' is given prominence in norm-referenced systems of assessment because of the practice of comparing performers in a cohort with one another, validity is of prime concern within criterion-referencing. Though the forms of evidence of competence may differ from candidate to candidate, what is important is their relevance and sufficiency to the purpose of demonstrating competence against the elements, as defined by NVQ range statements.

VERIFICATION

Defined as the process of monitoring carried out to ensure the accuracy of the process of assessment, verification is a major strength in NCVQ's quality assurance process. *Criteria* of assessment within the NVQ model are clearly expressed and subsequently elaborated through performance criteria and range statements. So too is the *process* of assessment and accreditation, which is systematically designed, rigorously implemented and monitored. A staged process for the accreditation of assessors involves the following functions:

● Accreditation of Prior Learning Adviser (D31)

● Accreditation of Prior Learning Assessor (D36)

● First Line Assessor (D32)

● Second Line Assessor (D32/33)

● Internal Verifier (at centre level) (D32/3/4)

● External Verifier (at awarding body level) (D32/3/4/5).

At each stage the possession of an appropriate NVQ qualification in assessment is required (shown in brackets).

SUMMARY

The NVQ model offers a quality approach to assessment, as support for learning, and therefore to the attainment of learning. It offers an assessment framework which is comprehensive and grounded in good practice and within which strategies that are seen to be conducive to optimizing learning relate to one another and flow logically from the adoption of 'outcomes'. Key features are:

● clear statements of learning outcome

● assessment and accreditation of prior learning

● access and progression through credit accumulation and transfer

- independence of mode of learning from the assessment requirements
- an open and equitable, demystified assessment process.

Finally, it is important to note that learners and learning, whatever their nature and contexts, are likely to be more purposive and effective if there are clear targets and outcomes on which to focus. It is also worth reminding ourselves, as participants within the teaching/learning process, that the optimal quality of the learning process is most likely when it is the learner who controls their own learning process. An outcomes-based approach to learning is conducive to both of these ends.

References

Abercrombie, MLJ (1989) *The Anatomy of Judgement: An investigation into the processes of perception and reasoning*, London: Free Association Books.

Atkins, MJ, Beattie, J and Dockrell, WB (1993) *Assessment Issues in Higher Education*, Sheffield: Employment Department.

Barnett, R (1994) *The Limits of Competence*, Buckingham: Open University Press/SRHE.

Baume, D and Brown, S (eds) (1992) *Learning Contracts, volume two, Some practical examples*, Birmingham: Standing Conference on Educational Development.

Becher, T (1989) *Academic Tribes and Territories*, Buckingham: SRHE and Open University Press.

Benne, KD, Bradford, LP and Lippett, R (1964) 'The laboratory method', in Bradford, L, Gibb JR and Benne, KD (eds) *T-Group Theory and Laboratory Method*, New York: John Wiley and Sons.

Bennett, RE and Ward, WC (eds) (1993) *Construction Versus Choice in Cognitive Measurement: Issues in constructed response, performance testing, and portfolio assessment*, Hillsdale, NJ: Lawrence Erlbaum Associates.

Berk, RA (1986) 'A consumer's guide to setting performance standards on criterion-referenced tests', *Review of Educational Research*, **56**, 137–72.

Bloom, BS (1956) *Taxonomy of Educational Objectives, volume 1, The cognitive domain*, London: Longman.

Boud, D (ed.) (1988a) *Developing Student Autonomy in Learning*, 2nd edn, London: Kogan Page.

Boud, D (1988b) 'Moving towards autonomy', in Boud, D (ed.) *Developing Student Autonomy in Learning*, 2nd edn, London: Kogan Page.

Boud, D (1991) *Implementing Student Self-Assessment, HERDSA Green Guide*, 2nd edn, Sydney: Higher Education Research and Development Society of Australasia.

Boud, D and Feletti, G (1992) *The Challenge of Problem Based Learning*, New York: San Martin's Press.

Brown, G and Pendlebury, M (1992) *Assessing Active Learning*, Sheffield,: CVCP Universities Staff Development and Training Unit.

Brown, S and Baume, D (eds) (1992) *Learning Contracts, volume one: A theoretical perspective*, Birmingham: Standing Conference on Educational Development.

Brown, S and Knight, P (1994) *Assessing Learners in Higher Education*, London: Kogan Page.

Brown, S, Rust, C and Gibbs, G (1994) *Strategies for Diversifying Assessment*, Oxford: Rewley Press.

Bruner, J (1970) 'Some theorems on instruction', in Stones, E (ed.) *Readings in Educational Psychology*, London: Methuen.

Bruner, J (1992) 'Another look at New Look 1', *American Psychologist*, **47**,6,780–83.

Channel Four (1993) 'All Our Futures – Britain's Education Revolution', London: Channel Four TV.

Dahlgren, L-O (1984) 'Outcomes of learning', in Marton, F, Hounsell, D and Entwistle, N (eds) *The Experience of Learning*, Edinburgh: Scottish Academic Press.

Ebel, RL and Frisbie, DA (1986) *Essentials of Educational Measurement*, Engelwood Cliffs, NJ: Prentice Hall.

Ecclestone, K (1994) 'Democratic values and purposes: the overlooked challenge of competence', *Journal of Educational Studies*, **20**, 2.

Eisner, EW (1993) 'Reshaping assessment in education: some criteria in search of practice', *Journal of Curriculum Studies*, **25**, 3, 219–33.

Elton, L *et al.* (1994) *Staff Development in Relation to Research*, Sheffield: CVCP Universities' Staff Development Unit.

English, L (1992) 'Children's use of domain-specific knowledge and domain-general strategies in novel problem solving', *British Journal of Educational Psychology*, **62**, 203–16.

Entwistle, NJ (1992) *The Impact of Teaching on Learning Outcomes in Higher Education*, Sheffield: Committee of Vice-Chancellors and Principals (Staff Development Unit).

Entwistle, NJ and Ramsden, P (1983) *Understanding Student Learning*, Beckenham: Croom Helm.

Entwistle, NJ and Entwistle, A (1991) 'Contrasting forms of understanding for degree examinations: the student experience and its implications', *Higher Education*, **22**, 205–27.

Eraut, M (1994a) *Ethics in Occupational Standards NVQs and SVQs*, Sheffield: Employment Department, Learning Methods Branch.

Eraut, M (1994b) *Developing Professional Knowledge and Competence*, London: Falmer Press.

Eraut, M and Cole, G (1993) 'Assessment of competence in higher level occupations', *Compendium No 3. Competence and Assessment*, Sheffield: Employment Department, Learning Methods Branch.

Erwin, T (1983) 'The scale of intellectual development: measuring Perry's scheme', *Journal of College Student Personnel*, **24**, 6–12.

Erwin, TD (1991) *Assessing Student Learning and Development*, San Francisco, CA: Jossey-Bass.

Falchikov, N (1986) 'Product comparisons and process benefits of collaborative self and peer group assessments', *Assessment and Evaluation in Higher Education*, **11**, 2, 146–66.

Falchikov, N (1988) 'Self and peer assessment of a group project designed to promote the skills of capability', *Programmed Learning and Educational Technology*, **25**, 4, 327–39.

Falchikov, N (submitted for publication) 'Peer Feedback Marking: developing peer assessment'.

Forehand, LS, Vann, WF and Shugars, DA (1982) 'Student self-evaluation in pre-clinical restorative dentistry', *Journal of Dental Education*, **46**, 4, 221–6.

Forster, F and Hounsell, D (1994) *Tutoring. A handbook for postgraduate and other part-time tutors*, Edinburgh: Centre for Teaching, Learning and Assessment.

Gibbs, G (1981) *Teaching Students to Learn*, Buckingham: Open University Press.

Gibbs, G (1991) 'Reflection and self assessment for new lecturers', in Brown, S and Dove, P (eds) *Self and Peer Assessment*, Birmingham: Staff and Educational Development Association.

Gibbs, G (1992) *Improving the Quality of Student Learning*, Bristol: Technical and Educational Services.

Gibbs, G (in press). 'Changing lecturers' conceptions of teaching and learning through action research', in Brew, A (ed.) *Directions in Staff Development*, Buckingham: SRHE/Open University Press.

Gibbs, G, Habeshaw, S and Habeshaw, T (1988) *53 Interesting Ways of Assessing Your Students*, 2nd edn, Bristol: Technical and Educational Services.

Gonczi, A (1994) 'Competency based assessment in the professions in Australia', *Assessment in Education*, **1**, 1, 27–44.

Gray, TGF (1987) 'An exercise in improving the potential of exams for learning', *European Journal of Engineering Education*, **12**, 4, 311–23.

Hager, P, Gonczi, A and Athanasou, J (1994) 'General issues about assessment of competence', *Assessment and Evaluation in Higher Education*, **19**, 1, 3–16.

Harvey, L (1993) 'An integrated approach to student assessment', Warwick: Paper presented to the Measure for Measure, Act II Conference, 6–8 September.

Hayes, E and Colin, SAJ (eds) (1994) *Confronting Sexism and Racism, New Directions for Adult and Continuing Education*, **61**, San Francisco, CA: Jossey-Bass.

Heron, J (1981) 'Assessment revisited', in Boud, D (ed.) *Developing Student Autonomy in Learning*, London: Kogan Page.

Heywood, J (1989) *Assessment in Higher Education*, 2nd edn, Chichester: John Wiley and Sons.

Hodkinson, P and Issitt, M (1994) *The Challenge of Competence*, London: Cassell.

Hounsell, D and Murray, R (1992) *Essay Writing for Active Learning*, Sheffield: CVCP Universities' Staff Development Unit.

Hustler, D, Peckett, J and Whiteley, M (1993) *Learning Contracts and Initial Professional Development: A case study from initial teacher education*, Manchester: Didsbury School of Education.

Hyland, T (1994) *Competence, Education and NVQs*, London: Cassell.

Jacobs, A (1974) 'The use of feedback in groups', in Jacobs, A and Spradlin, WW (eds) *The Group as Agent of Change*, New York: Behavioral Publications.

Jessup, G (1991) *Outcomes – NVQs and the emerging model of education and training*, London: Falmer Press.

Jordan, TE (1989) *Measurement and Evaluation in Higher Education*, London: Falmer Press.

Knight, P (ed.) (1994) *University-wide Change, Staff and Curriculum Development*, Birmingham: Staff and Educational Development Association.

Knight, P (1995) *Records of Achievement in Further and Higher Education*, Lancaster: Framework Press.

Knottenbelt, M and Fiddes, N (1994) *Part-Time Tutoring. A survey of teaching by postgraduate and other part-time tutors at the University of Edinburgh*, Edinburgh: Centre for Teaching, Learning and Assessment.

Knowles, M (1986) *Using Learning Contracts*, San Francisco, CA: Jossey Bass.

Kohn, A (1993) *Punished by Rewards*, Boston, Mass.: Houghton Mifflin.

Kolb, D (1984) *Experiential Learning*, Englewood Cliffs, NJ: Prentice Hall.

Korman, M and Stubblefield, RL (1971) 'Medical school evaluation and internship performance', *Journal of Medical Education*, **46**, 670–73.

Laurillard, DM (1984) 'Learning from problem solving', in Marton, F, Hounsell, D and Entwistle, N (eds), *The Experience of Learning*, Edinburgh: Scottish Academic Press.

Linn, BS, Arostegui, M and Zeppa, R (1975) 'Performance rating scale for peer and self assessments', *British Journal of Medical Education*, **9**, 98–101.

Linn, RL, Baker, EL and Dunbar, SB (1991) 'Complex, performance-based assessment: expectations and validation criteria', *Educational Researcher*, **20**, 8, 15–21.

Long, DG (1990) *Learner Managed Learning*, London: Kogan Page.

Luke, C and Gore, J (eds) (1992) *Feminisms and Critical Pedagogy*, London: Routledge.

MacDonald, RB (1991) 'Developmental students' processing of teacher feedback in composition instruction', *Review of Research in Developmental Education*, **8**, 5.

MacFarlane Report (1992) *Teaching and Learning in an Expanding Higher Education System*, Edinburgh: Committee of Scottish University Principals.

Marton, F and Saljo, R (1976) 'On qualitative differences in learning – outcomes as a function of the learner's conception of the task', *British Journal of Educational Psychology*, **46**, 115–27.

Marton, F and Saljo, R (1984) 'Approaches to learning', in Marton, F, Hounsell, D and Entwistle, N (eds) *The Experience of Learning*, Edinburgh: Scottish Academic Press.

Mast, TA and Bethart, H (1978) 'Evaluation of clinical dental procedures by senior dental students', *Journal of Dental Education*, **42**, 4, 196–7.

Mathews, BP (1994) 'Assessing individual contributions: experience of peer evaluation in major group projects', *British Journal of Educational Technology*, **5**, 1, 19–28.

Messick, S (1989) 'Validity', in Linn, RL (ed.) *Educational Measurement*, 3rd edn, New York: Macmillan.

Miller, CML and Parlett, M (1974) *Up to the Mark: A study of the examination game*, Guildford: SRHE.

Mitchell, L and Bartram, D (1994) *The Place of Knowledge and Understanding in the Development of National Vocational Qualifications and Scottish Vocational Qualifications*, Sheffield: Employment Department.

Morton, JB and Macbeth, WAAG (1977) 'Correlations between staff, peer, and self assessments of fourth-year students in surgery', *Medical Education*, **11**, 3, 167–70.

National Center for Education Statistics (1992) *National Assessment of College Student Learning: Issues and concerns*, Washington, DC: US Government Printing Office.

Osterlind, SJ (1989) *Constructing Test Items*, Norwell, MA: Kluwer Academic Publishers.

Otter, S (1992) *Learning Outcomes In Higher Education*, London: Department for Education.

Parry, M (1994) 'Renaissance virtue gets the soft sell', *The Times Higher Education Supplement*, 22 April, 22.

Perry, WG (1970) *Forms of Intellectual and Moral Development in the College Years: A scheme*, New York: Holt, Rinehart and Winston.

Pettit, P (ed.) (1993) *Consequentialism*, Aldershot: Dartmouth Publishing Co.

Pettman, JJ (1991) 'Towards a (personal) politics of location', *Studies in Continuing Education*, **13**, 2, 153–66.

Polytechnics and Colleges Funding Council/Council for National Academic Awards (1990) *The Measurement of Value Added in Higher Education*, London: CNAA.

Race, P (1992) 'Not a learning contract', in Brown and Baume, *op cit*.

Race, P (1994a) *The Open Learning Handbook*, 2nd edn, London: Kogan Page.

Race, P (1994b) *Never Mind the Teaching, Feel the Learning*, Birmingham: Staff and Educational Development Association.

Ramsden, P (1986) 'Students and quality', in Moodie, GC (ed.) *Standards and Criteria in Higher Education*, Guildford: SRHE and NFER-Nelson.

Ramsden, P (1987) 'Improving teaching and learning in higher education: the case for a relational perspective', *Studies in Higher Education*, **12**, 275–86.

Ramsden, P (1988) 'Studying learning: improving teaching', in Ramsden, P (ed.) *Improving Learning: New perspectives*, London: Kogan Page.

Rogers, CR (1983) *Freedom to Learn for the 80's*, Columbus, Ohio: Merrill.

Roid, GH and Haladyna, TM (1982) *A Technology for Test-Item Writing*, New York: Academic Press.

Rorty, R (1989) *Contingency, Irony and Solidarity*, Cambridge: Cambridge University Press.

Scriven, M (1967) 'The methodology of evaluation', in Tyler, RW *et al.* (eds) *Perspectives of Curriculum Evaluation*, Chicago: Rand McNally.

Stephenson, J and Laycock, M (eds) (1993) *Using Learning Contracts in Higher Education*, London: Kogan Page.

Stones, E (1970) 'Strategy and tactics in programmed instruction', in Stones, E (ed.) *Readings in Educational Psychology*, London: Methuen.

Terenzini, P (1993). 'Cross-national themes in the assessment of quality in higher education', *Assessment Update*, 5, 1–14.

Thomas, K (1990) *Gender and Subject in Higher Education*, Buckingham: SRHE/Open University Press.

Tomkins, C and McGraw, M-J (1988) 'The negotiated learning contract', in Boud, D (1988a), *op cit*.

Tomlinson, P and Saunders, S (1995) 'The current possibilities for competence profiling in teacher education', in Edwards, A and Knight, P (eds) *The Assessment of Competence in Higher Education*, London: Kogan Page.

Turner, K (1993) 'An investigation of how students respond to feedback on coursework', Warwick: Paper presented to the 'Measure for Measure Act II' Conference, September.

Wesman, AG (1972) 'Writing the test item', in Thorndike, RL (ed.) *Educational Measurement*, Washington, DC: American Council on Education.

Wiggins, G (1989) 'A true test: toward more authentic and equitable assessment', *Phi Delta Kappa*, **71**, 9, 703–13.

Winter, R (1995) 'The assessment of professional competences: the importance of general criteria', in Edwards, A and Knight, P (eds) *The Assessment of Competence in Higher Education*, London: Kogan Page.

Wood, R (1991) *Assessment and Testing*, Cambridge: Cambridge University Press.

Index